McDougal Littell Science

Ecology

symbiosis

Tickbird
(Buphagus erythrorhynchus)

Impala
(Aepyceros melampus)

LIFE SCIENCE

A ▶ Cells and Heredity
B ▶ Life Over Time
C ▶ Diversity of Living Things
D ▶ Ecology
E ▶ Human Biology

EARTH SCIENCE

A ▶ Earth's Surface
B ▶ The Changing Earth
C ▶ Earth's Waters
D ▶ Earth's Atmosphere
E ▶ Space Science

PHYSICAL SCIENCE

A ▶ Matter and Energy
B ▶ Chemical Interactions
C ▶ Motion and Forces
D ▶ Waves, Sound, and Light
E ▶ Electricity and Magnetism

Acknowledgments: Excerpts and adaptations from *National Science Education Standards* by the National Academy of Sciences. Copyright © 1996 by the National Academy of Sciences. Reprinted with permission from the National Academies Press, Washington, D.C.

Excerpts and adaptations from *Benchmarks for Science Literacy: Project 2061.* Copyright © 1993 by the American Association for the Advancement of Science. Reprinted with permission.

ISBN-13: 978-0-618-33429-2
ISBN-10: 0-618-33429-7   7 8 VJM 08 07 06
Internet Web Site: http://www.mcdougallittell.com

Science Consultants

Chief Science Consultant

James Trefil, Ph.D. is the Clarence J. Robinson Professor of Physics at George Mason University. He is the author or co-author of more than 25 books, including *Science Matters* and *The Nature of Science.* Dr. Trefil is a member of the American Association for the Advancement of Science's Committee on the Public Understanding of Science and Technology. He is also a fellow of the World Economic Forum and a frequent contributor to *Smithsonian* magazine.

Rita Ann Calvo, Ph.D. is Senior Lecturer in Molecular Biology and Genetics at Cornell University, where for 12 years she also directed the Cornell Institute for Biology Teachers. Dr. Calvo is the 1999 recipient of the College and University Teaching Award from the National Association of Biology Teachers.

Kenneth Cutler, M.S. is the Education Coordinator for the Julius L. Chambers Biomedical Biotechnology Research Institute at North Carolina Central University. A former middle school and high school science teacher, he received a 1999 Presidential Award for Excellence in Science Teaching.

Instructional Design Consultants

Douglas Carnine, Ph.D. is Professor of Education and Director of the National Center for Improving the Tools of Educators at the University of Oregon. He is the author of seven books and over 100 other scholarly publications, primarily in the areas of instructional design and effective instructional strategies and tools for diverse learners. Dr. Carnine also serves as a member of the National Institute for Literacy Advisory Board.

Linda Carnine, Ph.D. consults with school districts on curriculum development and effective instruction for students struggling academically. A former teacher and school administrator, Dr. Carnine also co-authored a popular remedial reading program.

Donald Steely, Ph.D. serves as principal investigator at the Oregon Center for Applied Science (ORCAS) on federal grants for science and language arts programs. His background also includes teaching and authoring of print and multimedia programs in science, mathematics, history, and spelling.

Sam Miller, Ph.D. is a middle school science teacher and the Teacher Development Liaison for the Eugene, Oregon, Public Schools. He is the author of curricula for teaching science, mathematics, computer skills, and language arts.

Vicky Vachon, Ph.D. consults with school districts throughout the United States and Canada on improving overall academic achievement with a focus on literacy. She is also co-author of a widely used program for remedial readers.

Content Reviewers

John Beaver, Ph.D.
Ecology
Professor, Director of Science Education Center
College of Education and Human Services
Western Illinois University
Macomb, IL

Donald J. DeCoste, Ph.D.
Matter and Energy, Chemical Interactions
Chemistry Instructor
University of Illinois
Urbana-Champaign, IL

Dorothy Ann Fallows, Ph.D., MSc
Diversity of Living Things, Microbiology
Partners in Health
Boston, MA

Michael Foote, Ph.D.
The Changing Earth, Life Over Time
Associate Professor
Department of the Geophysical Sciences
The University of Chicago
Chicago, IL

Lucy Fortson, Ph.D.
Space Science
Director of Astronomy
Adler Planetarium and Astronomy Museum
Chicago, IL

Elizabeth Godrick, Ph.D.
Human Biology
Professor, CAS Biology
Boston University
Boston, MA

Isabelle Sacramento Grilo, M.S.
The Changing Earth
Lecturer, Department of the Geological Sciences
San Diego State University
San Diego, CA

David Harbster, MSc
Diversity of Living Things
Professor of Biology
Paradise Valley Community College
Phoenix, AZ

Richard D. Norris, Ph.D.
Earth's Waters
Professor of Paleobiology
Scripps Institution of Oceanography
University of California, San Diego
La Jolla, CA

Donald B. Peck, M.S.
Motion and Forces; Waves, Sound, and Light;
Electricity and Magnetism
Director of the Center for Science Education (retired)
Fairleigh Dickinson University
Madison, NJ

Javier Penalosa, Ph.D.
Diversity of Living Things, Plants
Associate Professor, Biology Department
Buffalo State College
Buffalo, NY

Raymond T. Pierrehumbert, Ph.D.
Earth's Atmosphere
Professor in Geophysical Sciences (Atmospheric Science)
The University of Chicago
Chicago, IL

Brian J. Skinner, Ph.D.
Earth's Surface
Eugene Higgins Professor of Geology and Geophysics
Yale University
New Haven, CT

Nancy E. Spaulding, M.S.
Earth's Surface, The Changing Earth, Earth's Waters
Earth Science Teacher (retired)
Elmira Free Academy
Elmira, NY

Steven S. Zumdahl, Ph.D.
Matter and Energy, Chemical Interactions
Professor Emeritus of Chemistry
University of Illinois
Urbana-Champaign, IL

Susan L. Zumdahl, M.S.
Matter and Energy, Chemical Interactions
Chemistry Education Specialist
University of Illinois
Urbana-Champaign, IL

Safety Consultant

Juliana Texley, Ph.D.
Former K–12 Science Teacher and School Superintendent
Boca Raton, FL

English Language Advisor

Judy Lewis, M.A.
Director, State and Federal Programs for reading proficiency
and high risk populations
Rancho Cordova, CA

Teacher Panel Members

Carol Arbour
Tallmadge Middle School,
Tallmadge, OH

Patty Belcher
Goodrich Middle School,
Akron, OH

Gwen Broestl
Luis Munoz Marin Middle School,
Cleveland, OH

Al Brofman
Tehipite Middle School,
Fresno, CA

John Cockrell
Clinton Middle School,
Columbus, OH

Jenifer Cox
Sylvan Middle School,
Citrus Heights, CA

Linda Culpepper
Martin Middle School,
Charlotte, NC

Kathleen Ann DeMatteo
Margate Middle School,
Margate, FL

Melvin Figueroa
New River Middle School,
Ft. Lauderdale, FL

Doretha Grier
Kannapolis Middle School,
Kannapolis, NC

Robert Hood
Alexander Hamilton Middle School,
Cleveland, OH

Scott Hudson
Covedale Elementary School,
Cincinnati, OH

Loretta Langdon
Princeton Middle School,
Princeton, NC

Carlyn Little
Glades Middle School,
Miami, FL

Ann Marie Lynn
Amelia Earhart Middle School,
Riverside, CA

James Minogue
Lowe's Grove Middle School,
Durham, NC

Joann Myers
Buchanan Middle School,
Tampa, FL

Barbara Newell
Charles Evans Hughes Middle School,
Long Beach, CA

Anita Parker
Kannapolis Middle School,
Kannapolis, NC

Greg Pirolo
Golden Valley Middle School,
San Bernardino, CA

Laura Pottmyer
Apex Middle School,
Apex, NC

Lynn Prichard
Booker T. Washington Middle Magnet
School, Tampa, FL

Jacque Quick
Walter Williams High School,
Burlington, NC

Robert Glenn Reynolds
Hillman Middle School,
Youngstown, OH

Stacy Rinehart
Lufkin Road Middle School,
Apex, NC

Theresa Short
Abbott Middle School,
Fayetteville, NC

Rita Slivka
Alexander Hamilton Middle School,
Cleveland, OH

Marie Sofsak
B F Stanton Middle School,
Alliance, OH

Nancy Stubbs
Sweetwater Union Unified School District,
Chula Vista, CA

Sharon Stull
Quail Hollow Middle School,
Charlotte, NC

Donna Taylor
Okeeheelee Middle School,
West Palm Beach, FL

Sandi Thompson
Harding Middle School,
Lakewood, OH

Lori Walker
Audubon Middle School & Magnet Center,
Los Angeles, CA

Teacher Lab Evaluators

Andrew Boy
W.E.B. DuBois Academy,
Cincinnati, OH

Jill Brimm-Byrne
Albany Park Academy,
Chicago, IL

Gwen Broestl
Luis Munoz Marin Middle School,
Cleveland, OH

Al Brofman
Tehipite Middle School,
Fresno, CA

Michael A. Burstein
The Rashi School,
Newton, MA

Trudi Coutts
Madison Middle School,
Naperville, IL

Jenifer Cox
Sylvan Middle School,
Citrus Heights, CA

Larry Cwik
Madison Middle School,
Naperville, IL

Jennifer Donatelli
Kennedy Junior High School,
Lisle, IL

Melissa Dupree
Lakeside Middle School,
Evans, GA

Carl Fechko
Luis Munoz Marin Middle School,
Cleveland, OH

Paige Fullhart
Highland Middle School,
Libertyville, IL

Sue Hood
Glen Crest Middle School,
Glen Ellyn, IL

William Luzader
Plymouth Community Intermediate School,
Plymouth, MA

Ann Min
Beardsley Middle School,
Crystal Lake, IL

Aileen Mueller
Kennedy Junior High School,
Lisle, IL

Nancy Nega
Churchville Middle School,
Elmhurst, IL

Oscar Newman
Sumner Math and Science Academy,
Chicago, IL

Lynn Prichard
Booker T. Washington Middle Magnet
School, Tampa, FL

Jacque Quick
Walter Williams High School,
Burlington, NC

Stacy Rinehart
Lufkin Road Middle School,
Apex, NC

Seth Robey
Gwendolyn Brooks Middle School,
Oak Park, IL

Kevin Steele
Grissom Middle School,
Tinley Park, IL

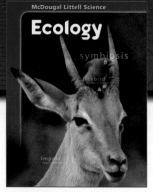

McDougal Littell Science

Ecology

symbiosis

blackbird

Impala

eEdition

Ecology

Unit Features

SCIENTIFIC AMERICAN

1 Ecosystems and Biomes   6

(the **BIG** idea)

Matter and energy together support life within an environment.

How many living and nonliving things can you identify in this photograph? page 6

How do living things interact? page 42

Features

Visual Highlights

Internet Resources @ ClassZone.com

INVESTIGATIONS AND ACTIVITIES

Standards and Benchmarks

Each chapter in **Ecology** covers some of the learning goals that are described in the *National Science Education Standards* (NSES) and the Project 2061 *Benchmarks for Science Literacy*. Selected content and skill standards are shown below in shortened form. The following National Science Education Standards are covered on pages xii–xxvii, in Frontiers in Science, and in Timelines in Science, as well as in chapter features and laboratory investigations: Understandings About Scientific Inquiry (A.9), Understandings About Science and Technology (E.6), Science and Technology in Society (F.5), Science as a Human Endeavor (G.1), Nature of Science (G.2), and History of Science (G.3).

Content Standards

1 Ecosystems and Biomes

National Science Education Standards

C.4.b	Food webs show how populations function as producers and consumers.
C.4.c	Most energy in ecosystems enters as sunlight, gets transferred into food by photosynthesis, and passes from organism to organism in food webs.
D.1.f	Water circulates through Earth's crust, oceans, and atmosphere.
D.3.d	The Sun is the major source of energy for growth of plants, winds, ocean currents, the water cycle, and seasonal variations.

Project 2061 Benchmarks

4.B.6	The water cycle occurs as water evaporates, condenses, falls, collects, and evaporates again.
5.A.1	Plants use sunlight to make food. Animals consume other organisms. Some living things don't fit either category.
5.A.5	All organisms are part of two connected food webs.
5.E.1	Food is obtained differently. Plants use sunlight, CO_2, and H_2O to make sugars. Some animals eat plants or other animals.
5.E.2	Matter is transferred between living things and the environment.
5.E.3	Energy can change form in living things.
11.A.1	A system can include processes as well as things.
11.A.2	In a system, every part relates. Output from one can become input to another.

2 Interactions Within Ecosystems

National Science Education Standards

C.1.a	The levels of organization in living systems are cells, organs, tissues, organ systems, organisms, and ecosystems.
C.4.a	An ecosystem is made of nonliving materials and populations.
C.4.d	Life in an ecosystem can be supported or limited by light, water, temperatures, soil, disease, or predators.

Project 2061 Benchmarks

5.D.1	Species with similar needs may compete for resources.
5.D.2	Types of living things may interact: as producer/consumer, predator/prey, parasite/host, or scavenger/decomposer or as cooperators or competitors for resources.
11.A.3	A system usually has subsystems and can be a subsystem of a larger system.
11.C.1	Systems change until stable, then remain stable until surroundings change.

Human Impact on Ecosystems

National Science Education Standards

E.6.d	All technology has risks and trade-offs, such as cost, safety, and efficiency.
E.6.e	All designs have limits, including availability, safety, and environmental impact.
F.1.g	Environmental health relies on monitoring.
F.2.a	Human overpopulation can cause • increased use of resources • decline in resources • decline in other populations
F.2.b	Causes of pollution and resource loss vary from place to place.

Project 2061 Benchmarks

3.C.5	New technologies can increase some risks and decrease others.
3.C.6	Technology issues are complex. Groups may have different values and priorities.
3.C.7	People control technology (and science) and are responsible for its effects.
4.B.8	Fresh water is necessary for life, limited in supply, used in industry, and becoming depleted and polluted.
4.B.10	The atmosphere and oceans cannot absorb all wastes.
4.C.7	Human activities have had environmental impacts.
6.E.5	The health of individuals requires taking steps to keep soil, air, and water safe.
8.A.3	In agriculture and all technology there is a trade-off between losses and gains.
8.C.3	Manufacturing needs an energy source.

Process and Skill Standards

National Science Education Standards

A.1	Identify questions that can be answered through scientific methods.
A.2	Design and conduct a scientific investigation.
A.3	Use appropriate tools and techniques to gather and analyze data.
A.4	Use evidence to describe, predict, explain, and model.
A.5	Think critically to find relationships between results and interpretations.
A.6	Give alternative explanations and predictions.
A.7	Communicate procedures and findings.
A.8	Use mathematics in scientific inquiry.

Project 2061 Benchmarks

9.A.2	Use negative numbers.
9.A.3	Write numbers in different forms.
9.B.2	Use mathematics to describe change.
9.B.3	Use graphs to show relationships.
11.B.1	Use models to think about processes.
11.C.4	Use equations to summarize changes.
11.D.2	With complex systems, use summaries, averages, ranges, and examples.
12.B.3	Calculate volumes of rectangular solids.
12.B.7	Determine, use, and convert units.
12.C.3	Use and read measurement instruments.
12.D.2	Read and interpret tables and graphs.
12.D.3	Research books, periodicals, databases.
12.D.4	Understand charts and graphs.
12.E.3	Be skeptical of biased samples.
12.E.4	See more than one way to interpret results.
12.E.5	Criticize faulty reasoning.

Introducing Life Science

Scientists are curious. Since ancient times, they have been asking and answering questions about the world around them. Scientists are also very suspicious of the answers they get. They carefully collect evidence and test their answers many times before accepting an idea as correct.

In this book you will see how scientific knowledge keeps growing and changing as scientists ask new questions and rethink what was known before. The following sections will help get you started.

What Is Life Science?

Life science is the study of living things. As you study life science, you will observe and read about a variety of organisms, from huge redwood trees to the tiny bacteria that cause sore throats. Because Earth is home to such a great variety of living things, the study of life science is rich and exciting.

But life science doesn't simply include learning the names of millions of organisms. It includes big ideas that help us to understand how all these living things interact with their environment. Life science is the study of characteristics and needs that all living things have in common. It's also a study of changes—both daily changes as well as changes that take place over millions of years. Probably most important, in studying life science, you will explore the many ways that all living things—including you—depend upon Earth and its resources.

The text and visuals in this book will invite you into the world of living things and provide you with the key concepts you'll need in your study. Activities offer a chance for you to investigate some aspects of life science on your own. The four unifying principles listed below provide a way for you to connect the information and ideas in this program.

- **All living things share common characteristics.**

- **All living things share common needs.**

- **Living things meet their needs through interactions with the environment.**

- **The types and numbers of living things change over time.**

the **BIG** idea

Each chapter begins with a big idea. Keep in mind that each big idea relates to one or more of the unifying principles.

All living things share common characteristics.

Birds nest among the plants of a reed marsh as sunlight shines and a breeze blows. Which of these is alive? Warblers and plants are living things, but sunlight and breezes are not. All living things share common characteristics that distinguish them from nonliving things.

What It Means

This unifying principle helps you explore one of the biggest questions in science, "What is life?" Let's take a look at four characteristics that distinguish living things from nonliving things: organization, growth, reproduction, and response.

Organization

If you stand a short distance from a reed warbler's nest, you can observe the largest level of organization in a living thing—the **organism** itself. Each bird is an organism. If you look at a leaf under a microscope, you can observe the smallest level of organization capable of performing all the activities of life, a **cell.** All living things are made of cells.

Growth

Most living things grow and develop. Growth often involves not only an increase in size, but also an increase in complexity, such as a tadpole growing into a frog. If all goes well, the small warblers in the picture will grow to the size of their parent.

Reproduction

Most living things produce offspring like themselves. Those offspring are also able to reproduce. That means that reed warblers produce reed warblers, which in turn produce more reed warblers.

Response

You've probably noticed that your body adjusts to changes in your surroundings. If you are exploring outside on a hot day, you may notice that you sweat. On a cold day, you may shiver. Sweating and shivering are examples of response.

Why It's Important

People of all ages experience the urge to explore and understand the living world. Understanding the characteristics of living things is a good way to start this exploration of life. In addition, knowing about the characteristics of living things helps you identify

• similarities and differences among various organisms
• key questions to ask about any organism you study

All living things share common needs.

What do you need to stay alive? What does an animal like a fish or a coral need to stay alive? All living things have common needs.

What It Means

Inside every living thing, chemical reactions constantly change materials into new materials. For these reactions to occur, an organism needs energy, water and other materials, and living space.

Energy

You use energy all the time. Movement, growth, and sleep all require energy, which you get from food. Plants use the energy of sunlight to make sugar for energy. Almost all animals get their energy by eating either plants or other animals that eat plants.

Water and Other Materials

Water is an important material in the cells of all living things. The chemical reactions inside cells take place in water, and water plays a part in moving materials around within organisms.

Other materials are also essential for life. For example, plants must have carbon dioxide from the air to make sugar. Plants and animals both use oxygen to release the energy stored in sugar. You and other animals that live on land get oxygen when you breathe in air. The fish swimming around the coral reef in the picture have gills, which allow them to get oxygen that is dissolved in the water.

Living Space

You can think of living space as a home—a space that protects you from external conditions and a place where you can get materials such as water and air. The ocean provides living space for the coral that makes up this coral reef. The coral itself provides living space for many other organisms.

Why It's Important

Understanding the needs of living things helps people make wise decisions about resources. This knowledge can also help you think carefully about
• the different ways in which various organisms meet their needs for energy and materials
• the effects of adding chemicals to the water and air around us
• the reasons why some types of plants or animals may disappear from an area

Living things meet their needs through interactions with the environment.

A moose chomps on the leaves of a plant. This ordinary event involves many interactions among living and nonliving things within the forest.

What It Means

To understand this unifying principle, take a closer look at the words *environment* and *interactions.*

Environment

The **environment** is everything that surrounds a living thing. An environment is made up of both living and nonliving factors. For example, the environment in this forest includes rainfall, rocks, and soil as well as the moose, the evergreen trees, and the birch trees. In fact, the soil in these forests is called "moose and spruce" soil because it contains materials provided by the animals and evergreens in the area.

Interaction

All living things in an environment meet their needs through interactions. An **interaction** occurs when two or more things act in ways that affect one another. For example, trees and other forest plants can meet their need for energy and materials through interactions with materials in soil and with air and light from the Sun. New plants get living space as birds, wind, and other factors carry seeds from one location to another.

Animals like this moose meet their need for food through interactions with other living things. The moose gets food by eating leaves off trees and other plants. In turn, the moose becomes food for wolves.

Why It's Important

Learning about living things and their environment helps scientists and decision makers address issues such as

- predicting how a change in the moose population would affect the soil in the forest
- determining the ways in which animals harm or benefit the trees in a forest
- developing land for human use without damaging the environment

The types and numbers of living things change over time.

The story of life on Earth is a story of changes. Some changes take place over millions of years. At one time, animals similar to modern fish swam in the area where this lizard now runs.

What It Means

To understand how living things change over time, let's look closely at the terms *diversity* and *adaptation*.

Diversity

You are surrounded by an astonishing variety of living things. This variety is called **biodiversity.** Today, scientists have described and named 1.4 million species. There are even more species that haven't been named. Scientists use the term *species* to describe a group of closely related living things. Members of a **species** are so similar that they can produce offspring that are able to reproduce. Lizards, such as the one you see in the photograph, are so diverse that they make up many different species.

Over the millions of years that life has existed on Earth, new species have originated and others have disappeared. The disappearance of a species is called **extinction.** Fossils, like the one in the photograph, provide evidence of some of the organisms that lived millions of years ago.

Adaptation

Scientists use the term **adaptation** to mean a characteristic of a species that allows members of that species to survive in a particular environment. Adaptations are related to needs. A lizard's legs are an adaptation that allows it to move on land.

Over time, species either develop adaptations to changing environments or they become extinct. The history of living things on Earth is related to the history of the changing Earth. The presence of a fishlike fossil indicates that the area shown in this photograph was once covered by water.

Why It's Important

By learning how living things change over time, you will gain a better understanding of the life that surrounds you and how it survives. Discovering more about the history of life helps scientists to

• identify patterns of relationships among various species
• predict how changes in the environment may affect species in the future

The Nature of Science

You may think of science as a body of knowledge or a collection of facts. More important, however, science is an active process that involves certain ways of looking at the world.

Scientific Habits of Mind

Scientists are curious. They are always asking questions. A scientist who observes that the number of plants in a forest preserve has decreased might ask questions such as, "Are more animals eating the plants?" or "Has the way the land is used affected the numbers of plants?" Scientists around the world investigate these and other important questions.

Scientists are observant. They are always looking closely at the world around them. A scientist who studies plants often sees details such as the height of a plant, its flowers, and how many plants live in a particular area.

Scientists are creative. They draw on what they know to form a possible explanation for a pattern, an event, or a behavior that they have observed. Then scientists create a plan for testing their ideas.

Scientists are skeptical. Scientists don't accept an explanation or answer unless it is based on evidence and logical reasoning. They continually question their own conclusions as well as conclusions suggested by other scientists. Scientists trust only evidence that is confirmed by other people or methods.

A white-tailed deer feeds on many plants, including the trillium shown here.

By measuring the growth of this tree, a scientist can study interactions in the ecosystem.

Science Processes at Work

You can think of science as a continuous cycle of asking and seeking answers to questions about the world. Although there are many processes that scientists use, scientists typically do each of the following:

• Observe and ask a question
• Determine what is known
• Investigate
• Interpret results
• Share results

Determine what is known → **Investigate** → **Interpret results** → **Share results** → **Ask a question** →

Observe and Ask a Question

It may surprise you that asking questions is an important skill. A scientific investigation may start when a scientist asks a question. Perhaps scientists observe an event or a process that they don't understand, or perhaps answering one question leads to another.

Determine What Is Known

When beginning an inquiry, scientists find out what is already known about a question. They study results from other scientific investigations, read journals, and talk with other scientists. A biologist who is trying to understand how the change in the number of deer in an area affects plants will study reports of censuses taken for both plants and animals.

Investigate

Investigating is the process of collecting evidence. Two important ways of collecting evidence are observing and experimenting.

Observing is the act of noting and recording an event, a characteristic, a behavior, or anything else detected with an instrument or with the senses. For example, a scientist notices that plants in one part of the forest are not thriving. She sees broken plants and compares the height of the plants in one area with the height of those in another.

An **experiment** is an organized procedure during which all factors but the one being studied are controlled. For example, the scientist thinks the reason some plants in the forest are not thriving may be that deer are eating the flowers off the plants. An experiment she might try is to mark two similar parts of an area where the plants grow and then build a fence around one part so the deer can't get to the plants there. The fence must be constructed so the same amounts of light, air, and water reach the plants. The only factor that changes is contact between plants and the deer.

Close observation of the Colorado potato beetle led scientists to a biological pesticide that can help farmers control this insect pest.

Forming hypotheses and making predictions are two other skills involved in scientific investigations. A **hypothesis** is a tentative explanation for an observation or a scientific problem that can be tested by further investigation. For example, since at least 1900, Colorado potato beetles were known to be resistant to chemical insecticides. Yet the numbers of beetles were not as large as expected. It was hypothesized that bacteria living in the beetles' environment were killing many beetles. A **prediction** is an expectation of what will be observed or what will happen and can be used to test a hypothesis. It was predicted that certain bacteria would kill Colorado potato beetles. This prediction was confirmed when a bacterium called *Bt* was discovered to kill Colorado potato beetles and other insect pests.

Interpret Results

As scientists investigate, they analyze their evidence, or data, and begin to draw conclusions. **Analyzing data** involves looking at the evidence gathered through observations or experiments and trying to identify any patterns that might exist in the data. Often scientists need to make additional observations or perform more experiments before they are sure of their conclusions. Many times scientists make new predictions or revise their hypotheses.

Computers help scientists analyze the sequence of base pairs in the DNA molecule.

Share Results

An important part of scientific investigation is sharing results of experiments. Scientists read and publish in journals and attend conferences to communicate with other scientists around the world. Sharing data and procedures gives them a way to test one another's results. They also share results with the public through newspapers, television, and other media.

Living things contain complex molecules such as RNA and DNA. To study them, scientists often use models like the one shown here.

The Nature of Technology

Imagine what life would be like without cars, computers, and cell phones. Imagine having no refrigerator or radio. It's difficult to think of a world without these items we call technology. Technology, however, is more than just machines that make our daily activities easier. Like science, technology is also a process. The process of technology uses scientific knowledge to design solutions to real-world problems.

Science and Technology

Science and technology go hand in hand. Each depends upon the other. Even designing a device as simple as a toaster requires knowledge of how heat flows and which materials are the best conductors of heat. Scientists also use a number of devices to help them collect data. Microscopes, telescopes, spectrographs, and computers are just a few of the tools that help scientists learn more about the world. The more information these tools provide, the more devices can be developed to aid scientific research and to improve modern lives.

The Process of Technological Design

Heart disease is among the leading causes of death today. Doctors have successfully replaced damaged hearts with hearts from donors. Medical engineers have developed pacemakers that improve the ability of a damaged heart to pump blood. But none of these solutions is perfect. Although it is very complex, the heart is really a pump for blood; thus, using technology to build a better replacement pump should be possible. The process of technological design involves many choices. In the case of an artificial heart, choices about how and what to develop involve cost, safety, and patient preference. What kind of technology will result in the best quality of life for the patient?

Identify a Need

Developers of technology must first establish exactly what needs their technology must meet. A healthy heart pumps blood at the rate of 5–30 liters per minute. What type of artificial pump could achieve such rates, responding to changes in activity level? Could such a pump be small enough to implant into a person? How would such a heart be powered? What materials would not be rejected by the human body?

Design and Develop

Several designs for artificial hearts have been proposed. The Jarvik-7 was the first intended to be a long-term replacement for a human heart. The Jarvik-7 did not work very well. Although it lengthened the lives of some patients, their quality of life was poor. Doctors and engineers knew they needed to refine the design further. For example, the heart needed to be smaller, and it needed to have a better power system. The heart also needed to be made out of a better material so that it would not cause blood clots when implanted into a patient.

Test and Improve

The new AbioCor heart may hold the solutions to many of these problems. This fully self-contained implantable device makes the goal of replacing a damaged heart seem not so far away. Still, many improvements will be needed before the AbioCor is routinely put into human beings. Tests of the AbioCor are still in progress.

Using McDougal Littell Science

Reading Text and Visuals

This book is organized to help you learn. Use these boxed pointers as a path to help you learn and remember the **Big Ideas** and **Key Concepts**.

Take notes.

Use the strategies on the **Getting Ready to Learn** page.

Read the Big Idea.

As you read **Key Concepts** for the chapter, relate them to **the Big Idea**.

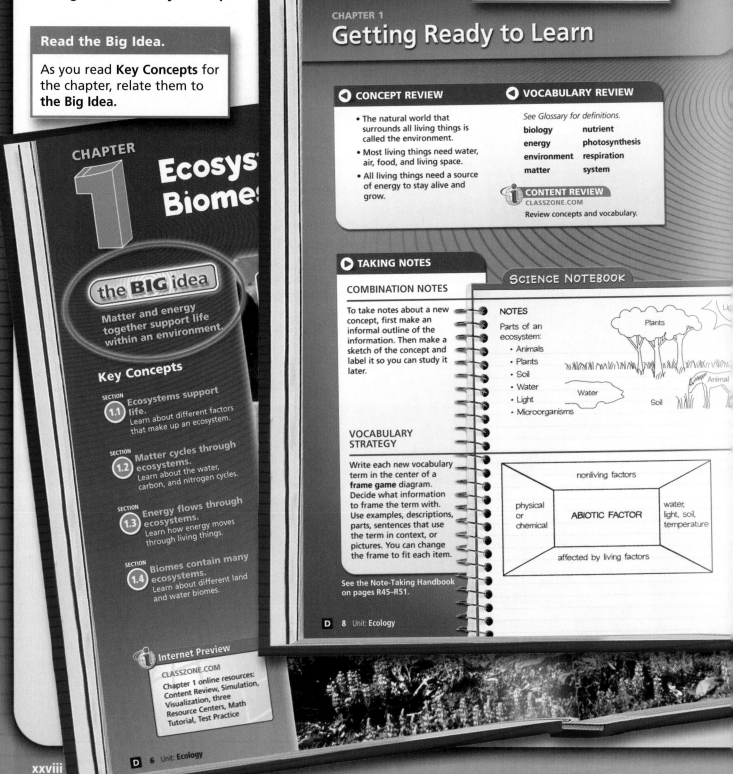

CHAPTER

1 Ecosys
Biome

the BIG idea

Matter and energy together support life within an environment.

Key Concepts

SECTION 1.1 Ecosystems support life.
Learn about different factors that make up an ecosystem.

SECTION 1.2 Matter cycles through ecosystems.
Learn about the water, carbon, and nitrogen cycles.

SECTION 1.3 Energy flows through ecosystems.
Learn how energy moves through living things.

SECTION 1.4 Biomes contain many ecosystems.
Learn about different land and water biomes.

Internet Preview

CLASSZONE.COM
Chapter 1 online resources: Content Review, Simulation, Visualization, three Resource Centers, Math Tutorial, Test Practice

D 6 Unit: Ecology

CHAPTER 1

Getting Ready to Learn

CONCEPT REVIEW

- The natural world that surrounds all living things is called the environment.
- Most living things need water, air, food, and living space.
- All living things need a source of energy to stay alive and grow.

VOCABULARY REVIEW

See Glossary for definitions.

biology   nutrient
energy   photosynthesis
environment   respiration
matter   system

CONTENT REVIEW
CLASSZONE.COM
Review concepts and vocabulary.

TAKING NOTES

COMBINATION NOTES

To take notes about a new concept, first make an informal outline of the information. Then make a sketch of the concept and label it so you can study it later.

VOCABULARY STRATEGY

Write each new vocabulary term in the center of a **frame game** diagram. Decide what information to frame the term with. Use examples, descriptions, parts, sentences that use the term in context, or pictures. You can change the frame to fit each item.

See the Note-Taking Handbook on pages R45–R51.

SCIENCE NOTEBOOK

NOTES
Parts of an ecosystem:
- Animals
- Plants
- Soil
- Water
- Light
- Microorganisms

Plants

Light

Water

Animal

Soil

nonliving factors

physical or chemical   ABIOTIC FACTOR   water, light, soil, temperature

affected by living factors

D 8 Unit: Ecology

Read each heading.

See how it fits in the outline of the chapter.

1.1 Ecosystems support life.

Remember what you know.

Think about concepts you learned earlier and preview what you'll learn now.

◀ **BEFORE, you learned**

- Living things need to obtain matter and energy from the environment
- The Sun provides Earth with light and heat

▶ **NOW, you will learn**

- What factors define an ecosystem
- About living factors in an ecosystem
- About nonliving factors in an ecosystem

VOCABULARY

ecology p. 9
ecosystem p. 9
biotic factor p. 10
abiotic factor p. 10

EXPLORE Your Environment

How much can temperature vary in one place?

PROCEDURE

① Choose three different locations inside your classroom where you can measure temperature.

② Place a thermometer at each location. Wait for at least two minutes. Record the temperatures in your notebook.

③ Compare the data you and your classmates have collected.

WHAT DO YOU THINK?

- Which location was the warmest, and which was the coldest?
- Describe what factors may have affected the temperature at each location.

MATERIALS

- thermometer
- stopwatch

Try the activities.

They will introduce you to science concepts.

Living things depend on the environment.

You wouldn't find a kangaroo in the Arctic and you won't see a polar bear in Australia. Each of these organisms is suited to a certain environment. The kangaroo and the polar bear are able to survive despite the harsh conditions of their surroundings. **Ecology** is the scientific study of how organisms interact with their environment and all the other organisms that live in that environment.

Scientists use the word **ecosystem** to describe a particular environment and all the living things that are supported by it. An ecosystem can be as small as a pond or as large as a desert. What is important in an ecosystem is how the living parts of the ecosystem relate to the nonliving parts.

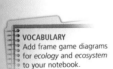

VOCABULARY
Add frame game diagrams for *ecology* and *ecosystem* to your notebook.

Learn the vocabulary.

Take notes on each term.

Chapter 1: **Ecosystems and Biomes** 9 **D**

Reading Text and Visuals

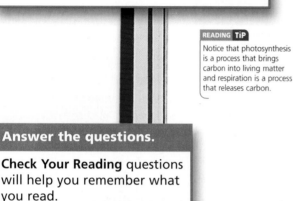

Read one paragraph at a time.

Look for a topic sentence that explains the main idea of the paragraph. Figure out how the details relate to that idea. One paragraph might have several important ideas; you may have to reread to understand.

READING TiP

Notice that photosynthesis is a process that brings carbon into living matter and respiration is a process that releases carbon.

Answer the questions.

Check Your Reading questions will help you remember what you read.

Study the visuals.

- Read the title.
- Read all labels and captions.
- Figure out what the picture is showing. Notice colors, arrows, and lines.

Carbon cycles through ecosystems.

Carbon is an element found in all living things. Carbon moves through Earth's ecosystems in a cycle referred to as the **carbon cycle**. It is through carbon dioxide gas found in Earth's atmosphere that carbon enters the living parts of an ecosystem.

Plants use carbon dioxide to produce sugar—a process called photosynthesis. Sugars are carbon compounds that are important building blocks in food and all living matter. Food supplies the energy and materials living things need to live and grow. To release the energy in food, organisms break down the carbon compounds—a process called respiration. Carbon is released and cycled back into the atmosphere as carbon dioxide. When living things die and decay, the rest of the carbon that makes up living matter is released.

CHECK YOUR READING Name three ways that living things are part of the carbon cycle.

Earth's oceans contain far more carbon than the air does. In water ecosystems—lakes, rivers, and oceans—carbon dioxide is dissolved in water. Algae and certain types of bacteria are the photosynthetic organisms that produce food in these ecosystems. Marine organisms, too, release carbon dioxide during respiration. Carbon is also deposited on the ocean floor when organisms die.

Carbon Cycle

Different processes combine to move carbon through the environment.

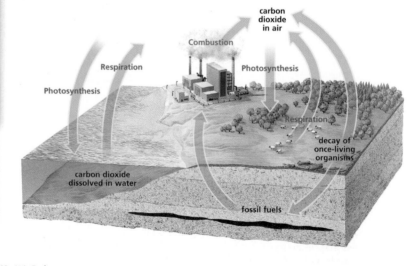

carbon dioxide in air

Combustion

Respiration

Photosynthesis

Photosynthesis

Respiration

decay of once-living organisms

carbon dioxide dissolved in water

fossil fuels

D 18 Unit: Ecology

Doing Labs

To understand science, you have to see it in action. Doing labs helps you understand how things really work.

① Read the entire lab first.

② Form a hypothesis.

③ Follow the procedure.

④ Record the data.

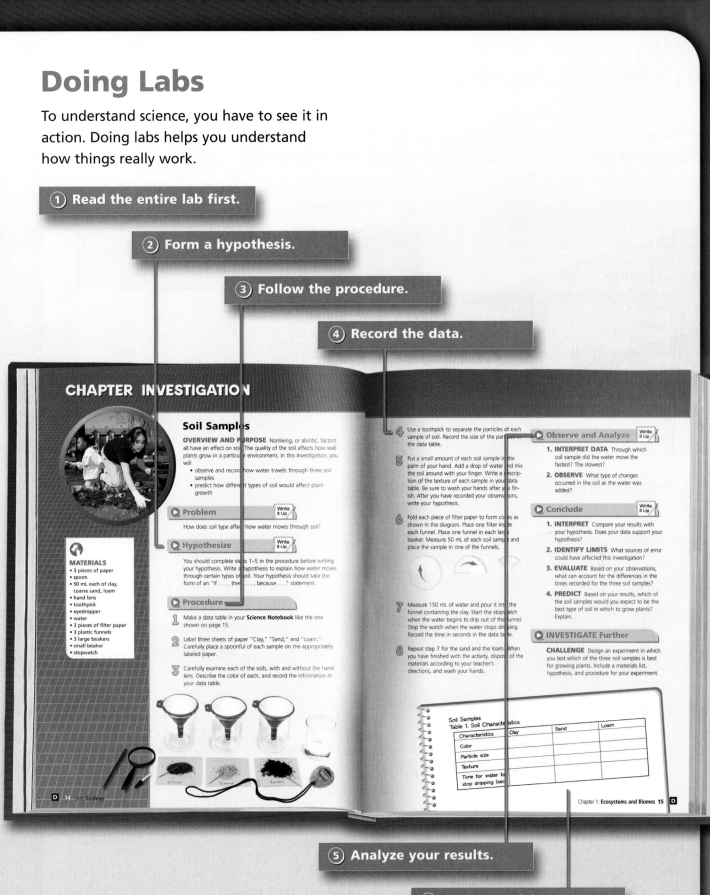

CHAPTER INVESTIGATION

Soil Samples

OVERVIEW AND PURPOSE Nonliving, or abiotic, factors all have an effect on soil. The quality of the soil affects how well plants grow in a particular environment. In this investigation, you will
- observe and record how water travels through three soil samples
- predict how different types of soil would affect plant growth

Problem · Write It Up

How does soil type affect how water moves through soil?

Hypothesize · Write It Up

You should complete steps 1–5 in the procedure before writing your hypothesis. Write a hypothesis to explain how water moves through certain types of soil. Your hypothesis should take the form of an "If . . . , then . . . , because . . ." statement.

Procedure

1. Make a data table in your **Science Notebook** like the one shown on page 15.

2. Label three sheets of paper "Clay," "Sand," and "Loam." Carefully place a spoonful of each sample on the appropriately labeled paper.

3. Carefully examine each of the soils, with and without the hand lens. Describe the color of each, and record the information in your data table.

MATERIALS
- 3 pieces of paper
- spoon
- 50 mL each of clay, coarse sand, loam
- hand lens
- toothpick
- eyedropper
- water
- 3 pieces of filter paper
- 3 plastic funnels
- 3 large beakers
- small beaker
- stopwatch

4. Use a toothpick to separate the particles of each sample of soil. Record the size of the particles in the data table.

5. Put a small amount of each soil sample in the palm of your hand. Add a drop of water and mix the soil around with your finger. Write a description of the texture of each sample in your data table. Be sure to wash your hands after you finish. After you have recorded your observations, write your hypothesis.

6. Fold each piece of filter paper to form cones as shown in the diagram. Place one filter inside each funnel. Place one funnel in each large beaker. Measure 50 mL of each soil sample and place the sample in one of the funnels.

7. Measure 150 mL of water and pour it into the funnel containing the clay. Start the stopwatch when the water begins to drip out of the funnel. Stop the watch when the water stops dripping. Record the time in seconds in the data table.

8. Repeat step 7 for the sand and the loam. When you have finished with the activity, dispose of the materials according to your teacher's directions, and wash your hands.

Observe and Analyze · Write It Up

1. **INTERPRET DATA** Through which soil sample did the water move the fastest? The slowest?

2. **OBSERVE** What type of changes occurred in the soil as the water was added?

Conclude · Write It Up

1. **INTERPRET** Compare your results with your hypothesis. Does your data support your hypothesis?

2. **IDENTIFY LIMITS** What sources of error could have affected this investigation?

3. **EVALUATE** Based on your observations, what can account for the differences in the times recorded for the three soil samples?

4. **PREDICT** Based on your results, which of the soil samples would you expect to be the best type of soil in which to grow plants? Explain.

INVESTIGATE Further

CHALLENGE Design an experiment in which you test which of the three soil samples is best for growing plants. Include a materials list, hypothesis, and procedure for your experiment.

Soil Samples
Table 1. Soil Characteristics

Characteristics	Clay	Sand	Loam
Color			
Particle size			
Texture			
Time for water to stop dripping (sec)			

D 14 Unit: Ecology

Chapter 1: Ecosystems and Biomes 15 D

⑤ Analyze your results.

⑥ Write your lab report.

Using Technology

The Internet is a great source of information about up-to-date science. The ClassZone Web site and SciLinks have exciting sites for you to explore. Video clips and simulations can make science come alive.

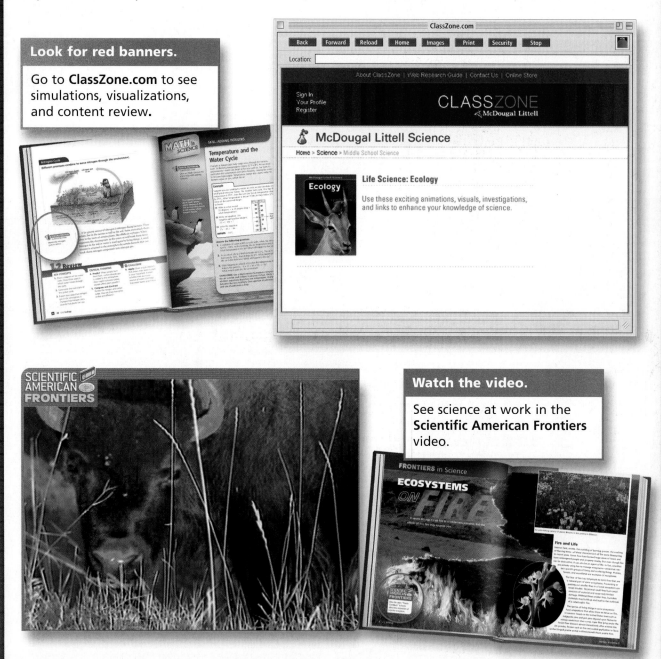

Look for red banners.

Go to **ClassZone.com** to see simulations, visualizations, and content review.

Watch the video.

See science at work in the **Scientific American Frontiers** video.

Look up SciLinks.

Go to **scilinks.org** to explore the topic.

Food Chains and Food Webs **CODE: MDL001**

Ecology
Contents Overview

Unit Features

1 Ecosystems and Biomes   6

the BIG idea

Matter and energy together support life
within an environment.

2 Interactions Within Ecosystems   42

the BIG idea

Living things within an ecosystem interact with
each other and the environment.

3 Human Impact on Ecosystems   78

the BIG idea

Humans and human population growth
affect the environment.

ECOSYSTEMS ON FIRE

It may seem strange to set fire to a wilderness preserve, but fire brings health to some ecosystems.

SCIENTIFIC
AMERICAN
FRONTIERS

View the video "Prairie Comeback" to learn about the restoration of a prairie ecosystem.

An astonishing variety of plants blooms in this prairie in Missouri.

Fire and Life

Intense heat, smoke, the crackling of burning grasses, the crashing of flaming trees—all these characteristics of fire seem threatening. In recent years, forest fires have burned huge areas of forest and have endangered people and property nearby. But even though fire can be destructive, it can also be an agent of life. In fact, scientists are actively using fire to manage ecosystems—areas that contain specific groups of living and nonliving things. Prairies, forests, and woodlands are examples of ecosystems.

The fear of fire has led people to limit fires that are a natural part of some ecosystems. Preventing or putting out smaller fires in a forest ecosystem can mean trouble. Occasional small fires burn small amounts of material and cause only limited damage. Without these smaller fires, burnable materials may build up and lead to the outbreak of a catastrophic fire.

The species of living things in some ecosystems have adaptations that allow them to thrive on fire. In North America trees such as lodgepole pine and jack pine depend upon flames to release seeds from their cones. Cape lilies lying under the forest floor blossom almost immediately after a forest fire. On prairies, flowers such as the rare coastal gayfeather in Texas or the fringed prairie orchid in Illinois benefit from prairie fires.

Seven months after a controlled burn, light shines on a new patch of wild hyacinth growing at the base of an oak tree.

Observing Patterns

Ecosystems include living things, such as plants and animals, and nonliving things, such as water and soil. Fires affect both the living and the nonliving. The photographs above show part of an oak woodland ecosystem. The photograph on the left shows a burn—a fire set deliberately by humans. The photograph on the right shows the same area seven months later.

Ashes left from fires add nutrients to the soil. Fire also opens space on the forest floor. Areas that were shaded by small trees, plants, and dead branches receive light. Over time, wild hyacinth and other new plants grow around the oak, and new insects and animals move into the area.

View the "Prairie Comeback" segment of your Scientific American Frontiers video to see how understanding ecosystems can help bring a prairie into bloom.

IN THIS SCENE FROM THE VIDEO ▶ a bison grazes on new growth that appears after the prairie is burned.

BRINGING BACK THE PRAIRIE At one time natural events, such as lightning, along with human activity caused regular patterns of fire on the prairie. Bison grazed on tender young plants that grew up after fires, and the plants that weren't eaten by the bison had room to grow. In 1989, an organization called The Nature Conservancy turned the Chapman-Barnard Cattle Ranch in Northeast Oklahoma into the Tall Grass Prairie Restoration Preserve.

Scientists at the preserve are using controlled fire and reintroducing bison to the area. Today there are more than 750 species of plants and animals growing in the preserve.

In tall-grass prairie ecosystems, fire provides similar benefits. Fire burns away overgrown plants, enriches the soil, and clears the way for the growth of new plants. Bison prefer to graze on these new plants that appear after a fire.

A New Understanding

Although some of the benefits provided by ecosystems can't be measured, researchers are starting to measure the financial contributions of ecosystems. Ecosystems may help clean our water, balance gases in the atmosphere, and maintain temperature ranges.

Researchers today are studying these benefits. In fact, a new frontier in ecology, called ecosystem services, is emerging. This new study is gaining the attention of both scientists and economists.

Given our growing awareness of the importance of ecosystems, should humans deliberately set fire to areas in forests or prairies? The answer to this question requires an understanding of interactions among living and nonliving parts of ecosystems. Forest and prairie fires can be dangerous, but properly managed, they provide important benefits to society as well as to the natural world.

UNANSWERED Questions

Understanding the connections within ecosystems raises more questions. In the coming years, people will need to analyze the costs and benefits of ecosystem restoration.

- How will humans balance the need to feed the human population with the cost of destroying ecosystems such as the prairie?
- How can scientists and wildlife managers protect people and property near forests while maintaining forest ecosystems?
- How do ecosystems protect natural resources, such as soil and water?

UNIT PROJECTS

As you study this unit, work alone or with a group on one of the projects listed below. Use the bulleted steps to guide your project.

Build an Ecosystem

Use an aquarium or other container to build an ecosystem.

- Set up your ecosystem. Observe it daily, and record your observations.
- Bring your ecosystem into your classroom, or take photographs and make diagrams of it. Present the record of your observations along with the visual displays.

Conservation Campaign

Find out how much water, paper, and energy are used in a month at your school.

- Describe a plan for conserving resources.
- Present your plan. You might make posters, write announcements, or perform a short skit.

Design a Park

You are part of a group that is planning a park near your school. Your group wants the park to include plants that lived in the area twenty-five years ago.

- Collect information from local museums, park districts, or botanic gardens. You can also visit Web sites sponsored by those organizations.
- Prepare a report and drawing of your park design.

CAREER CENTER
CLASSZONE.COM

Learn more about careers in ecology.

1

Ecosystems and Biomes

the **BIG** idea

Matter and energy together support life within an environment.

Key Concepts

SECTION

1.1 **Ecosystems support life.**
Learn about different factors that make up an ecosystem.

SECTION

1.2 **Matter cycles through ecosystems.**
Learn about the water, carbon, and nitrogen cycles.

SECTION

1.3 **Energy flows through ecosystems.**
Learn how energy moves through living things.

SECTION

1.4 **Biomes contain many ecosystems.**
Learn about different land and water biomes.

Internet Preview

CLASSZONE.COM

Chapter 1 online resources: Content Review, Simulation, Visualization, three Resource Centers, Math Tutorial, Test Practice

How many living and nonliving things can you identify in this photograph?

EXPLORE (the **BIG** idea)

How Do Plants React to Sunlight?

Move a potted plant so that the Sun shines on it from a different direction. Observe the plant each day for a week.

Observe and Think What change do you observe in the plant? What is it that plants get from the Sun?

What Is Soil?

Get a cupful of soil from outside and funnel it into a clear plastic bottle. Fill the bottle two-thirds full with water and place the bottle cap on tightly. Shake the bottle so that the soil and water mix completely. Place the bottle on a windowsill overnight. Wash your hands.

Observe and Think What has happened to the soil and water mixture? How many different types of material do you observe?

Internet Activity: A Prairie Ecosystem

Go to **ClassZone.com** to discover the types of plants and animals best adapted for tall-grass and short-grass prairies. Learn more about how to keep a prairie thriving.

Observe and Think What do all prairie plants have in common? How do prairie plants differ?

NSTA scilinks.org
SCi*LINKS*

Food Chains and Food Webs **Code: MDL001**

CHAPTER 1

Getting Ready to Learn

CONCEPT REVIEW

- The natural world that surrounds all living things is called the environment.
- Most living things need water, air, food, and living space.
- All living things need a source of energy to stay alive and grow.

VOCABULARY REVIEW

See Glossary for definitions.

biology
energy
environment
matter
nutrient
photosynthesis
respiration
system

CONTENT REVIEW
CLASSZONE.COM
Review concepts and vocabulary.

TAKING NOTES

COMBINATION NOTES

To take notes about a new concept, first make an informal outline of the information. Then make a sketch of the concept and label it so you can study it later.

VOCABULARY STRATEGY

Write each new vocabulary term in the center of a **frame game** diagram. Decide what information to frame the term with. Use examples, descriptions, parts, sentences that use the term in context, or pictures. You can change the frame to fit each item.

See the Note-Taking Handbook on pages R45–R51.

SCIENCE NOTEBOOK

NOTES

Parts of an ecosystem:
- Animals
- Plants
- Soil
- Water
- Light
- Microorganisms

Light
Plants
Animal
Water
Soil

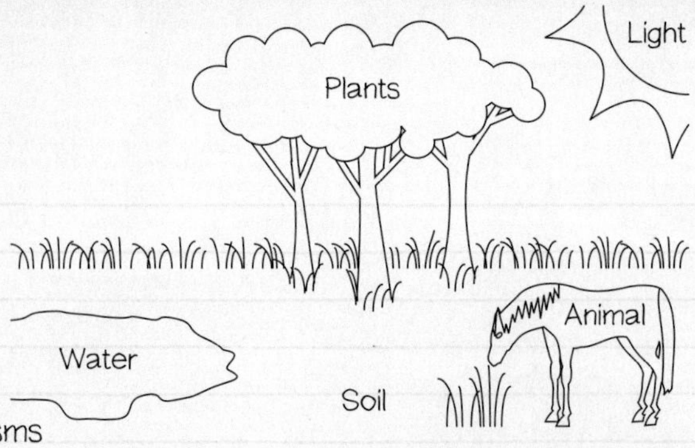

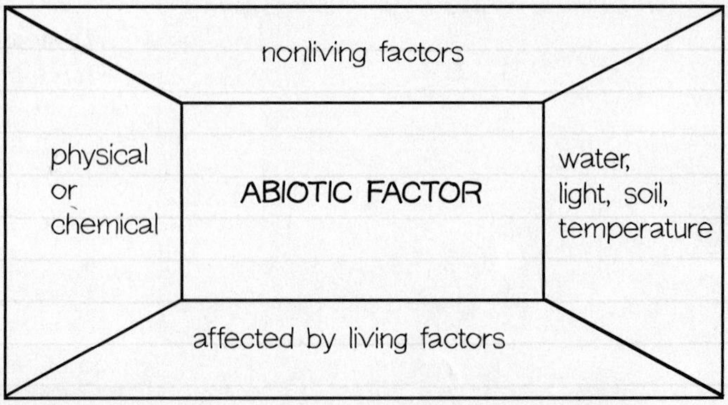

nonliving factors
physical or chemical
ABIOTIC FACTOR
water, light, soil, temperature
affected by living factors

1.1 Ecosystems support life.

◀ BEFORE, you learned

- Living things need to obtain matter and energy from the environment
- The Sun provides Earth with light and heat

▶ NOW, you will learn

- What factors define an ecosystem
- About living factors in an ecosystem
- About nonliving factors in an ecosystem

VOCABULARY

ecology p. 9
ecosystem p. 9
biotic factor p. 10
abiotic factor p. 10

EXPLORE Your Environment

How much can temperature vary in one place?

PROCEDURE

① Choose three different locations inside your classroom where you can measure temperature.

② Place a thermometer at each location. Wait for at least two minutes. Record the temperatures in your notebook.

③ Compare the data you and your classmates have collected.

WHAT DO YOU THINK?

- Which location was the warmest, and which was the coldest?
- Describe what factors may have affected the temperature at each location.

MATERIALS

- thermometer
- stopwatch

VOCABULARY
Add frame game diagrams for *ecology* and *ecosystem* to your notebook.

Living things depend on the environment.

You wouldn't find a kangaroo in the Arctic and you won't see a polar bear in Australia. Each of these organisms is suited to a certain environment. The kangaroo and the polar bear are able to survive despite the harsh conditions of their surroundings. **Ecology** is the scientific study of how organisms interact with their environment and all the other organisms that live in that environment.

Scientists use the word **ecosystem** to describe a particular environment and all the living things that are supported by it. An ecosystem can be as small as a pond or as large as a desert. What is important in an ecosystem is how the living parts of the ecosystem relate to the nonliving parts.

Let's take a look at a pond. A pond ecosystem is more than just water and fish. Plants grow in and around the water, and animals feed on these plants. A variety of tiny microorganisms in the water are food for fish and for each other. These are just a few of the living parts, or **biotic factors** (by-AHT-ihk), of a pond ecosystem. The nonliving parts, or **abiotic factors** (AY-by-AHT-ihk), include the air that supplies oxygen and carbon dioxide, the soil that provides nutrients, the water in the pond, and the sunlight that plants need to grow.

CLASSIFY Name three living and three nonliving factors that are part of this pond ecosystem.

Biotic factors interact with an ecosystem.

Living things depend upon an ecosystem for food, air, and water, as well as other things they need for survival. In turn, living things have an impact on the ecosystem in which they live. Plants, as a biotic factor in land ecosystems, affect other biotic and abiotic parts of ecosystems. Plants are an important source of food. The types of plants found in a particular ecosystem will determine the types of animals that can live there. Plants can affect temperature by blocking sunlight. Plant roots hold soil in place. Even the atmosphere is affected by plants taking in carbon dioxide and releasing oxygen.

Animals, as biotic factors, also affect an ecosystem. A beaver that builds a dam changes the flow of a river and so affects the surrounding landscape. Large herds of cattle can overgraze a grassland ecosystem and cause the soil to erode. In an ocean biome, corals form giant reefs that provide food and shelter for marine organisms.

Many abiotic factors affect ecosystems.

Abiotic factors include both the physical and chemical parts of an ecosystem. Physical factors are factors that you can see or feel, such as the temperature or the amount of water or sunlight. Important chemical factors include the minerals and compounds found in the soil and whether the ecosystem's water is fresh or salty. It is the combination of different abiotic factors that determines the types of organisms that an ecosystem will support.

READING TiP
The word *biotic* means "living." The prefix *a-* in *abiotic* means "not," so *abiotic* means "not living."

 CHECK YOUR READING List four different abiotic factors that can affect an ecosystem.

Temperature

Temperature is an important abiotic factor in any ecosystem. In a land ecosystem, temperature affects the types of plants that will do well there. The types of plants available for food and shelter, in turn, determine the types of animals that can live there. For example, a tropical rain forest has not only a lot of rain but it has consistently warm temperatures. The wide variety of plants that grow in a tropical rain forest supports a wide variety of monkeys, birds, and other organisms.

Animals are as sensitive to temperature as plants are. Musk oxen with their thick coat of fur can survive in very cold environments, where temperatures of −40°C (−40°F) are normal. The water buffalo, with its light coat, is better suited to warm temperatures. The wild water buffalo lives where temperatures can reach 48°C (118°F).

This musk ox's thick fur keeps it warm in the cold temperatures of northern Canada.

A water buffalo cools itself in a shallow stream during a hot day in India.

READING VISUALS COMPARE AND CONTRAST How are these animals alike? How are they different?

COMBINATION NOTES
Remember to make notes and diagrams to show how abiotic factors affect biotic factors in an ecosystem.

Light

You can easily understand how abiotic factors work together when you think about sunlight and temperature. Sunlight warms Earth's surface and atmosphere. In addition, energy from sunlight supports all life on Earth. The Sun provides the energy that plants capture and use to produce food in a process called photosynthesis. The food produced by plants, and other photosynthetic organisms, feeds almost all the other living things found on Earth.

The strength of sunlight and the amount of sunlight available in a land ecosystem determine the types of plants in that ecosystem. A desert ecosystem will have plants like cacti, which can survive where sunlight is very strong. Meanwhile, mosses and ferns grow well on the forest floor, where much of the light is blocked by the trees above.

Light is a factor in ocean ecosystems as well. The deeper the water is, the less light there is available. In the shallow water near the shore, photosynthetic organisms can survive at the surface and on the ocean floor. In the open ocean, light is available for photosynthetic organisms only in the first hundred meters below the surface.

Soil

Soil, which is a mixture of small rock and mineral particles, is an important abiotic factor in land ecosystems. Organisms within the soil break down the remains of dead plants and animals. This process of decay provides important raw materials to the living plants and animals of an ecosystem.

The size of soil particles affects how much air and water the soil can hold.

decayed leaves

earthworm

roots

Different ecosystems have different types of soil. The characteristics of the soil in an ecosystem affect plant growth. Soils that have a lot of decaying, or organic, matter can hold water well and allow air to reach the plant roots. Sandy soils usually do not hold water well because the water flows through too easily. Clay soil, which has small, tightly packed particles, will not allow water to move through easily at all. Minerals in the soil also affect plant growth.

 CHECK YOUR READING Explain how soil can affect plant life in an ecosystem.

Water

Another important abiotic factor in land ecosystems is the amount of water available to support life. All living things need water to carry out life processes. Plants need water as well as sunlight for photosynthesis. Animals need water to digest food and release the energy stored in the food. Look at the photograph to see the effect that an underground water source has on an otherwise dry, desert ecosystem. Trees could not survive there without a plentiful supply of water.

Ecosystems that have a lot of water can support a large number of different types of plants. These different types of plants can then support a large number of different types of animals. Tropical rain forests, the wettest of all ecosystems on land, are also the most diverse. Desert ecosystems, which are the driest land ecosystems, have far fewer types of plants and animals. The types and number of living things in a land ecosystem will always be related to the amount of fresh water available for its inhabitants.

INFER An oasis forms in the desert when underground water comes to the surface. How can you identify the boundary of this oasis?

1.1 Review

KEY CONCEPTS

1. Draw a diagram of an ecosystem near where you live. Label the factors "biotic" or "abiotic."

2. Give two examples of how plants and animals affect their environment.

3. Describe how temperature, light, and soil affect an ecosystem.

CRITICAL THINKING

4. **Predict** Think of a forest ecosystem. Now imagine that a large volcanic eruption throws large amounts of dust and ash into the air, blocking out sunlight. How might the forest ecosystem be affected if the sunlight is blocked for a day? For a year?

CHALLENGE

5. **Apply** Think of how you fit into your local environment. List ways in which you interact with biotic and abiotic factors within your ecosystem.

CHAPTER INVESTIGATION

Soil Samples

OVERVIEW AND PURPOSE Nonliving, or abiotic, factors all have an effect on soil. The quality of the soil affects how well plants grow in a particular environment. In this investigation, you will

- observe and record how water travels through three soil samples
- predict how different types of soil would affect plant growth

▶ Problem

How does soil type affect how water moves through soil?

▶ Hypothesize

You should complete steps 1–5 in the procedure before writing your hypothesis. Write a hypothesis to explain how water moves through certain types of soil. Your hypothesis should take the form of an "If . . . , then . . . , because . . ." statement.

▶ Procedure

1. Make a data table in your **Science Notebook** like the one shown on page 15.

2. Label three sheets of paper "Clay," "Sand," and "Loam." Carefully place a spoonful of each sample on the appropriately labeled paper.

3. Carefully examine each of the soils, with and without the hand lens. Describe the color of each, and record the information in your data table.

MATERIALS
- 3 pieces of paper
- spoon
- 50 mL each of clay, coarse sand, loam
- hand lens
- toothpick
- eyedropper
- water
- 3 pieces of filter paper
- 3 plastic funnels
- 3 large beakers
- small beaker
- stopwatch

4 Use a toothpick to separate the particles of each sample of soil. Record the size of the particles in the data table.

5 Put a small amount of each soil sample in the palm of your hand. Add a drop of water and mix the soil around with your finger. Write a description of the texture of each sample in your data table. Be sure to wash your hands after you finish. After you have recorded your observations, write your hypothesis.

6 Fold each piece of filter paper to form cones as shown in the diagram. Place one filter inside each funnel. Place one funnel in each large beaker. Measure 50 mL of each soil sample and place the sample in one of the funnels.

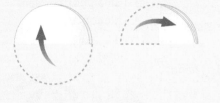

7 Measure 150 mL of water and pour it into the funnel containing the clay. Start the stopwatch when the water begins to drip out of the funnel. Stop the watch when the water stops dripping. Record the time in seconds in the data table.

8 Repeat step 7 for the sand and the loam. When you have finished with the activity, dispose of the materials according to your teacher's directions, and wash your hands.

▶ Observe and Analyze   Write It Up

1. **INTERPRET DATA** Through which soil sample did the water move the fastest? The slowest?

2. **OBSERVE** What type of changes occurred in the soil as the water was added?

▶ Conclude   Write It Up

1. **INTERPRET** Compare your results with your hypothesis. Does your data support your hypothesis?

2. **IDENTIFY LIMITS** What sources of error could have affected this investigation?

3. **EVALUATE** Based on your observations, what can account for the differences in the times recorded for the three soil samples?

4. **PREDICT** Based on your results, which of the soil samples would you expect to be the best type of soil in which to grow plants? Explain.

▶ INVESTIGATE Further

CHALLENGE Design an experiment in which you test which of the three soil samples is best for growing plants. Include a materials list, hypothesis, and procedure for your experiment.

Soil Samples
Table 1. Soil Characteristics

Characteristics	Clay	Sand	Loam
Color			
Particle size			
Texture			
Time for water to stop dripping (sec)			

1.2 Matter cycles through ecosystems.

◄ BEFORE, you learned

- Ecosystems support life
- Living and nonliving factors interact in an ecosystem
- Temperature, light, soil, and water are important nonliving factors in ecosystems

► NOW, you will learn

- How matter is exchanged between organisms and their environment
- About the water, carbon, and nitrogen cycles

VOCABULARY

cycle p. 16
water cycle p. 17
carbon cycle p. 18
nitrogen cycle p. 19

EXPLORE The Water Cycle

Do plants release water?

PROCEDURE

① Cover a branch of the plant with a plastic bag. Tape the bag firmly around the stem.

② Water the plant and place it in a sunny window or under a lamp. Wash your hands.

③ Check the plant after ten minutes, at the end of class, and again the next day.

WHAT DO YOU THINK?
- What do you see inside the plastic bag?
- What purpose does the plastic bag serve?

MATERIALS
- 1 small potted plant
- 1 clear plastic bag
- tape
- water

All ecosystems need certain materials.

RESOURCE CENTER
CLASSZONE.COM

Explore cycles in nature.

Living things depend on their environment to meet their needs. You can think of those needs in terms of the material, or matter, required by all living things. For example, all organisms take in water and food in order to survive. All of the materials an organism takes in are returned to the ecosystem, while the organism lives or after it dies.

The movement of matter through the living and nonliving parts of an ecosystem is a continuous process, a cycle. A **cycle** is a series of events that happens over and over again. Matter in an ecosystem may change form, but it never leaves the ecosystem, so the matter is said to cycle through the ecosystem. Three of the most important cycles in ecosystems involve water, carbon, and nitrogen.

Different processes combine to move water through the environment.

Precipitation
Condensation
water vapor in air
Respiration
Transpiration
runoff
Evaporation
groundwater

Water cycles through ecosystems.

Water is stored on Earth's surface in lakes, rivers, and oceans. Water is found underground, filling the spaces between soil particles and cracks in rocks. Large amounts of water are stored in glaciers and polar ice sheets. Water is also part of the bodies of living things. But water is not just stored, it is constantly moving. The movement of water through the environment is called the **water cycle.**

Water is made up of just two elements: oxygen and hydrogen. As water moves through an ecosystem, it changes in physical form, moving back and forth between gas, liquid, and solid. Water in the atmosphere is usually in gaseous form—water vapor. Water that falls to Earth's surface is referred to as precipitation. For precipitation to occur, water vapor must condense—it must change into a liquid or solid. This water can fall as rain, snow, sleet, mist, or hail.

CHECK YOUR READING What are the three physical forms of water in the water cycle?

Water returns to the atmosphere when heated, changing back into vapor, a process called evaporation. Living things also release water vapor. Animals release water vapor when they breathe, or respire. Plants release water vapor through a process called transpiration.

COMBINATION NOTES
Make notes and draw a diagram to show how water cycles through ecosystems.

Carbon cycles through ecosystems.

Carbon is an element found in all living things. Carbon moves through Earth's ecosystems in a cycle referred to as the **carbon cycle.** It is through carbon dioxide gas found in Earth's atmosphere that carbon enters the living parts of an ecosystem.

READING TiP

Notice that photosynthesis is a process that brings carbon into living matter and respiration is a process that releases carbon.

Plants use carbon dioxide to produce sugar—a process called photosynthesis. Sugars are carbon compounds that are important building blocks in food and all living matter. Food supplies the energy and materials living things need to live and grow. To release the energy in food, organisms break down the carbon compounds—a process called respiration. Carbon is released and cycled back into the atmosphere as carbon dioxide. When living things die and decay, the rest of the carbon that makes up living matter is released.

CHECK YOUR READING Name three ways that living things are part of the carbon cycle.

Earth's oceans contain far more carbon than the air does. In water ecosystems—lakes, rivers, and oceans—carbon dioxide is dissolved in water. Algae and certain types of bacteria are the photosynthetic organisms that produce food in these ecosystems. Marine organisms, too, release carbon dioxide during respiration. Carbon is also deposited on the ocean floor when organisms die.

Carbon Cycle

Different processes combine to move carbon through the environment.

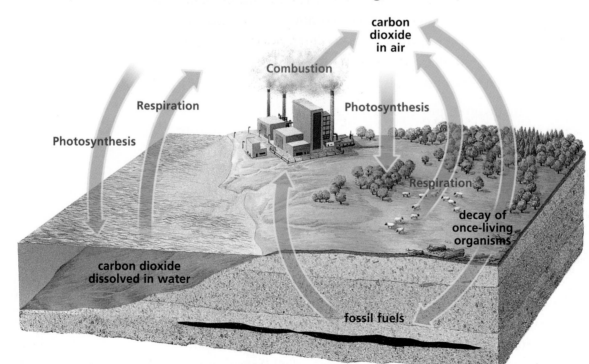

carbon dioxide in air

Combustion

Respiration

Photosynthesis

Photosynthesis

Respiration

decay of once-living organisms

carbon dioxide dissolved in water

fossil fuels

What is one form in which carbon is stored on the ocean floor?

PROCEDURE

1. Use the mortar and pestle to crush the seashell into a powder.

2. Pour the powder into a small beaker.

3. Add enough white vinegar to cover the powder.

WHAT DO YOU THINK?

- What happens when white vinegar is added to the crushed shell?

- What is the material produced in the reaction and where did it come from originally?

CHALLENGE What type of reaction have you observed?

SKILL FOCUS
Observing

MATERIALS
- mortar and pestle
- whole seashell or fragments
- small beaker
- white vinegar

TIME
15 minutes

Large amounts of carbon are stored underground. The remains of plants and animals buried for millions of years decay slowly and change into fossil fuels, such as coal and oil. The carbon in fossil fuels returns to ecosystems in a process called combustion. As humans burn fossil fuels to release energy, dust particles and gases containing carbon are also released into the environment.

Nitrogen cycles through ecosystems.

Nitrogen is another element important to life that cycles through Earth in the **nitrogen cycle.** Almost four-fifths of the air you breathe is clear, colorless nitrogen gas. Yet, you cannot get the nitrogen you need to live from the air. All animals must get nitrogen from plants.

Plants cannot use pure nitrogen gas either. However, plants can absorb certain compounds of nitrogen. Plants take in these nitrogen compounds through their roots, along with water and other nutrients. So how does the nitrogen from the atmosphere get into the soil? One source is lightning. Every lightning strike breaks apart, or fixes, pure nitrogen, changing it into a form that plants can use. This form of nitrogen falls to the ground when it rains.

Nitrogen Cycle

Different processes combine to move nitrogen through the environment.

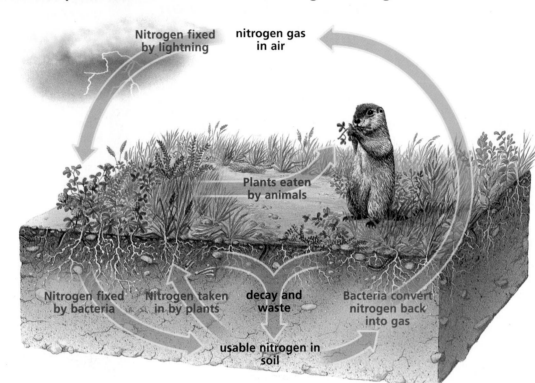

Nitrogen fixed by lightning

nitrogen gas in air

Plants eaten by animals

Nitrogen fixed by bacteria

Nitrogen taken in by plants

decay and waste

Bacteria convert nitrogen back into gas

usable nitrogen in soil

VISUALIZATION
CLASSZONE.COM

Watch the nitrogen cycle in action.

A far greater source of nitrogen is nitrogen-fixing bacteria. These bacteria live in the oceans as well as the soil. Some even attach themselves to the roots of certain plants, like alfalfa or soybeans. When organisms die, decomposers in the ocean or soil break them down. Nitrogen in the soil or water is used again by living things. A small amount is returned to the atmosphere by certain bacteria that can break down nitrogen compounds into nitrogen gas.

1.2 Review

KEY CONCEPTS

1. Draw a diagram of the water cycle. Show three ways in which water moves through the cycle.

2. Summarize the main parts of the carbon cycle.

3. Explain two ways that nitrogen gas in the atmosphere is changed into nitrogen compounds that plants can use.

CRITICAL THINKING

4. **Predict** When people burn fossil fuels, carbon dioxide gas is added to the atmosphere. How might increased carbon dioxide affect plant growth?

5. **Compare and Contrast** Review the nitrogen and carbon cycles. How are these two cycles similar and different?

CHALLENGE

6. **Apply** Draw a cycle diagram that shows how water is used in your household. Include activities that use water, sources of water, and ways that water leaves your house.

MATH TUTORIAL
CLASSZONE.COM

Click on Math Tutorial for more help with adding integers.

This iceberg is made up of fresh water, which freezes at 0°C. The surrounding ocean is salt water, which doesn't freeze at 0°C.

Temperature and the Water Cycle

Changes in temperature help water move through the environment. At freezing temperatures—below 32°F or 0°C for sea-level environments—water can begin to become solid ice. Ice starts to melt when the temperature rises above freezing, causing the water to become liquid again. Temperature change also causes water to become vapor, or gas, within the air.

Example

Suppose you are waiting for winter to come so you can skate on a small pond near your house. The weather turns cold. One day the temperature is 25°C, then the next day the air temperature drops by 35°C. What temperature is the air? If the air stays below 0°C, some of the water will begin to freeze.

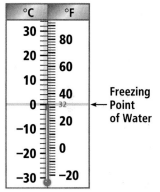

(1) Write a verbal model:
25 degrees + a 35-degree drop = what temperature?

(2) Write an equation. Use negative and positive integers:
$25 + (-35) = ?$

(3) Solve the equation:
$25 - 35 = -10$

ANSWER -10°C.

Answer the following questions.

1. A container of water is left out over night, when the temperature is -18°C. In the morning, the air temperature rises by 8°C. What temperature is the air? What will happen to the water?

2. An ice block sits in a field where the air is 0°C. The air temperature rises by 16°C, then it drops by 8°C. What temperature is the air in the field now? What will happen to the ice?

3. What happens to a block of ice after the temperature in the air follows this pattern: $-6 + 17 + 10 + 18 + (-5)$? What temperature has the air reached?

CHALLENGE Use a thermometer to measure the temperature of the air outside and indoors in degrees Celsius. Write two addition equations that show the temperature change between the two locations. One equation should show a rise, and one should show a drop.

1.3 Energy flows through ecosystems.

◀ BEFORE, you learned

- Matter cycles continuously through an ecosystem
- Living things are part of the water, carbon, and nitrogen cycles

▶ NOW, you will learn

- How living things move energy through an ecosystem
- How feeding relationships are important in ecosystems
- How the amount of energy changes as it flows through an ecosystem

VOCABULARY

producer p. 23
consumer p. 24
decomposer p. 25
food chain p. 26
food web p. 26
energy pyramid p. 28

EXPLORE Energy

How can you observe energy changing form?

PROCEDURE

1. Mark and cut a spiral pattern in a square piece of paper.

2. Cut a 15-cm piece of thread and tape one end to the center of the spiral.

3. Adjust the lamp to shine straight at the ceiling. Turn the lamp on.

4. Hold the spiral by the thread and let it hang 10 cm above the light bulb. CAUTION: Don't let the paper touch the bulb!

MATERIALS

- paper
- marker
- scissors
- thread
- tape
- desk lamp

WHAT DO YOU THINK?

- What do you see happen to the spiral?
- In what sense has the energy changed form?

Living things capture and release energy.

Everything you do—running, reading, and working—requires energy. The energy you use is chemical energy, which comes from the food you eat. When you go for a run, you use up energy. Some of that energy is released to the environment as heat, as you sweat. Eventually, you will need to replace the energy you've used.

Energy is vital to all living things. Most of that energy comes either directly or indirectly from the Sun. To use the Sun's energy, living things must first capture that energy and store it in some usable form. Because energy is continuously used by the activities of living things, it must be continuously replaced in the ecosystem.

Producers

All of these producers capture energy from sunlight.

Plants

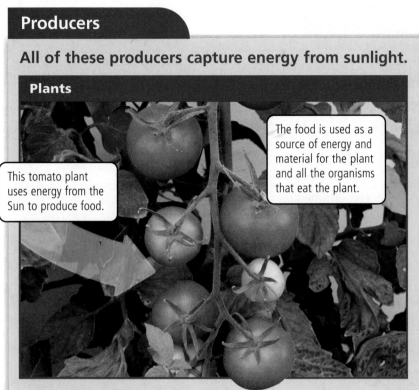

This tomato plant uses energy from the Sun to produce food.

The food is used as a source of energy and material for the plant and all the organisms that eat the plant.

READING VISUALS What process do all of these producers have in common?

Seaweed

Seaweed is a producer found in Earth's oceans and coastal zones.

Phytoplankton

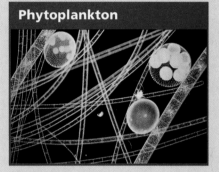

The most numerous producers are tiny organisms that live in water called phytoplankton.

Producers

A **producer** is an organism that captures energy and stores it in food as chemical energy. The producers of an ecosystem make energy available to all the other living parts of an ecosystem. Most energy enters ecosystems through photosynthesis. Plants, and other photosynthetic organisms, take water and carbon dioxide from their environment and use energy from the Sun to produce sugars. The chemical energy stored in sugars can be released when sugars are broken down.

VOCABULARY Remember to add a frame game for *producers* to your notebook.

CHECK YOUR READING How does energy enter into the living parts of an ecosystem?

Plants are the most common producers found in land ecosystems. In water ecosystems, most food is produced by photosynthetic bacteria and algae. A few examples of producers that use photosynthesis are shown in the photographs above.

The Sun provides most of the energy that is stored in food. One exception is the unusual case of a type of bacteria that lives in the deep ocean, where there is no sunlight. These bacteria produce food using heated chemicals released from underwater vents. This process is called chemosynthesis. Whether producers use photosynthesis or chemosynthesis, they do just as their name suggests—they produce food for themselves and for the rest of the ecosystem.

Consumers

A consumer is an organism that gets energy by eating producers or other consumers.

Producer: tree

Primary consumer: caterpillar

Secondary consumer: bird

READING VISUALS How does the energy inside the leaf get transferred to the bird?

Consumers

Organisms that cannot produce their own food must get their food from other sources. **Consumers** are organisms that get their energy by eating, or consuming, other organisms. To understand how energy flows through an ecosystem, you have to study feeding relationships. A feeding relationship starts with a producer, followed by one and often many more consumers.

CHECK YOUR READING Describe the producer-consumer relationship in terms of energy.

READING TiP

Primary is a word that means "first in order," *secondary* means "second in order," and *tertiary* means "third in order."

Consumers are classified by their position in a feeding relationship. In a meadow ecosystem, animals such as antelopes and grasshoppers feed on grasses. They are primary consumers because they are the first link between the producers and the rest of the consumers in an ecosystem. The wolves that eat the antelopes and the meadowlarks that eat the grasshoppers are secondary consumers. There are also tertiary consumers, like the prairie falcon that eats the meadowlark. Ecosystems also have special consumers called scavengers, like the vulture, which is a consumer that feeds on dead animals.

In the photograph above, energy enters the ecosystem through the tree, which is the producer. The caterpillar that gets its energy by feeding on the leaves is the first, or primary, consumer. The bird that gets its energy by feeding on the caterpillar is a secondary consumer.

Decomposers

If you've been for a hike through a forest, or a walk through a park, you have seen the interaction of producers and consumers. Tall trees and leafy shrubs are home to many insects and the birds that feed upon the insects. Also important to the maintenance of an ecosystem are decomposers, a group of organisms that often go unseen. **Decomposers** are organisms that break down dead plant and animal matter into simpler compounds.

mushrooms

Fungi, such as these mushrooms, are decomposers.

You can think of decomposers as the clean-up crew of an ecosystem. In a forest, consumers such as deer and insects eat a tiny fraction of the leaves on trees and shrubs. The leaves that are left on the forest floor, as well as dead roots and branches, are eventually digested by fungi and bacteria living in the soil. Decomposers also break down animal remains, including waste materials. A pinch of soil may contain almost half a million fungi and billions of bacteria.

The energy within an ecosystem gets used up as it flows from organism to organism. Decomposers are the organisms that release the last bit of energy from once-living matter. Decomposers also return matter to soil or water where it may be used again and again.

INVESTIGATE Decomposers

Where do decomposers come from?

PROCEDURE

1. Carefully use scissors to cut an opening across the middle of the bottle.

2. Place a handful of stones in the bottom of the bottle for drainage, and add enough soil to make a layer 10 cm deep.

3. Place some leaves and fruit slices on top of the soil.

WHAT DO YOU THINK?

- What do you observe happening to the fruit slices?
- Where do the decomposers in your bottle come from?

CHALLENGE Predict what would happen if you used potting soil instead of soil from outside.

4. Seal the cut you made with tape. Mark the date on the tape.

5. Add water through the top of the bottle to moisten the soil, and put the cap on the bottle. Wash your hands.

6. Observe the fruit slices each day for two weeks. Record your observations. Keep the soil moist.

October 3

SKILL FOCUS
Observing

MATERIALS
- clear soda bottle with cap
- scissors
- stones
- garden soil
- leaves
- slices of fruit
- masking tape
- marker
- water

TIME
30 minutes

Models help explain feeding relationships.

COMBINATION NOTES
Remember to take notes and draw a diagram for *food chain* and *food web*.

You have learned how energy is captured by producers and moved through ecosystems by consumers and decomposers. Scientists use two different models to show the feeding relationships that transfer energy from organism to organism. These models are food chains and food webs.

Food Chain

A chain is made of links that are connected one by one. Scientists use the idea of links in a chain as a model for simple feeding relationships. A **food chain** describes the feeding relationship between a producer and a single chain of consumers in an ecosystem.

The illustration in the white box on page 27 shows a wetland food chain. The first link in the chain is a cattail, a primary producer that captures the Sun's energy and stores it in food. The second link is a caterpillar, a primary consumer of the cattail. The frog is the next link, a secondary consumer that eats the caterpillar. The final link is a heron, a tertiary consumer that eats the frog. Energy is captured and released at each link in the chain. The arrows represent the flow of energy from organism to organism. You can see that some of the energy captured by the cattail makes its way through a whole chain of other organisms in the ecosystem.

Food Web

A **food web** is a model of the feeding relationships between many different consumers and producers in an ecosystem. A food web is more like a spiderweb, with many overlapping and interconnected food chains. It is a better model for the complex feeding relationships in an ecosystem, which usually has many different producers, with many primary and secondary consumers.

The illustration on page 27 also shows a wetland food web. You can see that the feeding relationships can go in several directions. For example, the food web shows that ruddy ducks eat bulrushes, which are producers. That makes ruddy ducks primary consumers. Ruddy ducks are also secondary consumers because they eat snails. A food web shows how one consumer can play several roles in an ecosystem.

READING TiP

Notice that the food chain described above is also a part of the food web described here. Follow the blue arrows in the diagram on page 27.

 CHECK YOUR READING What is the difference between a food chain and a food web?

Both food chains and food webs show how different organisms receive their energy. They also show how different organisms depend on one another. If one organism is removed from the food web or food chain, it may affect many other organisms in the ecosystem.

Energy Flows Through Ecosystems

Energy is transferred from one organism to the next as organisms eat or are eaten.

A Wetland Food Chain

Flow of Energy
Energy flow starts at the bottom. Arrows represent energy moving from an organism that is eaten to the organism that eats it.

A Wetland Food Web

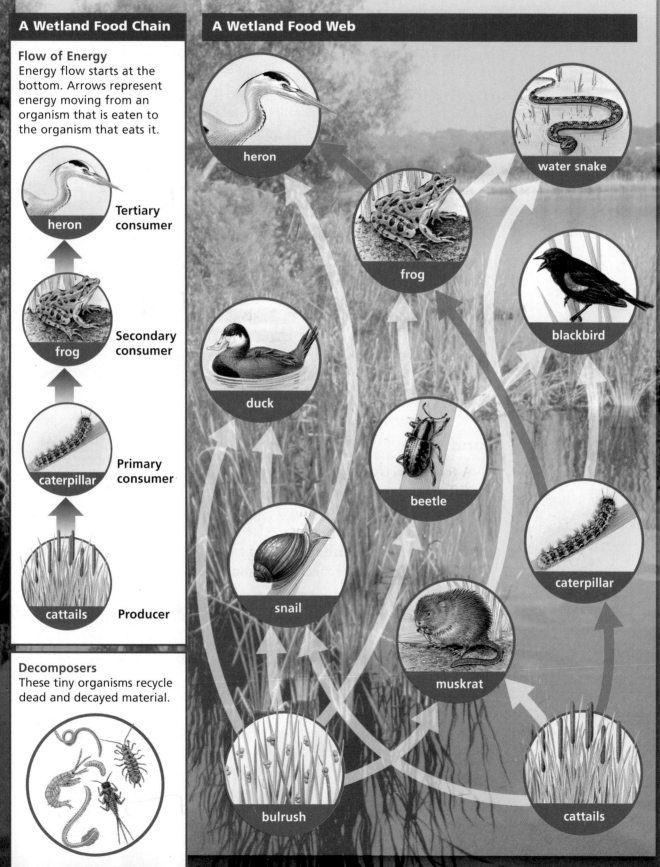

heron — Tertiary consumer

frog — Secondary consumer

caterpillar — Primary consumer

cattails — Producer

Decomposers
These tiny organisms recycle dead and decayed material.

heron

water snake

frog

duck

blackbird

beetle

caterpillar

snail

muskrat

bulrush

cattails

Available energy decreases as it moves through an ecosystem.

Another way to picture the flow of energy in an ecosystem is to use an energy pyramid. An **energy pyramid** is a model that shows the amount of energy available at each feeding level of an ecosystem. The first level includes the producers, the second level the primary consumers, and so on. Because usable energy decreases as it moves from producers to consumers, the bottom level is the largest. The available energy gets smaller and smaller the farther up the pyramid you go.

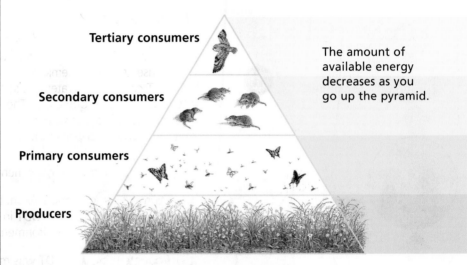

Tertiary consumers

The amount of available energy decreases as you go up the pyramid.

Secondary consumers

Primary consumers

Producers

READING TiP
Refer to the diagram above as you read the text. It is because available energy decreases at each level that the diagram takes the shape of a pyramid.

In the pyramid shown here, plants are the producers. They capture energy from sunlight, use some of it, then store the rest as food. The plants are eaten by insects, which also use some of the energy before being eaten by shrews. The shrews use energy before being eaten by the owl. You can see that it takes a lot of sunlight to support the producers and consumers in a food web that feeds an owl.

1.3 Review

KEY CONCEPTS

1. Describe the role of producers, consumers, and decomposers in an ecosystem.

2. Explain why a food web provides a better model of an ecosystem than a food chain does.

3. Explain how the amount of available energy changes as energy moves up a food chain.

CRITICAL THINKING

4. **Apply** Draw a food chain and a food web for an ecosystem near your home.

5. **Predict** Imagine that muskrats are removed from a wetland ecosystem. Predict what would happen both to producers and to secondary consumers.

⚫ CHALLENGE

6. **Synthesize** Explain how the carbon cycle is related to a food web. Describe how energy and matter move through the food web and the carbon cycle.

Biomagnification

Matter moves through living things in an ecosystem. Some of it is used up, some of it is stored. Sometimes, a toxic, or poisonous, material can get into a food chain and be stored. Biomagnification is the process by which matter becomes concentrated in living things.

Moving up the Food Chain

DDT provides one example of the effects of biomagnification in an ecosystem. DDT is a chemical that was widely used to kill plant-eating insects. Some chemicals break down over time, but DDT does not. DDT collected in water and soil, was absorbed by living things, and moved up the food chain. The diagram shows how DDT became magnified in a wetland ecosystem. It entered through tiny organisms called zooplankton, which absorbed DDT from the water.

1. The concentration of DDT in zooplankton was about 800 times greater than in the environment.

2. Minnows fed on zooplankton. DDT was magnified 31 times, so the concentration of DDT in minnows was 24,800 times greater than in the environment: 800 x 31 = 24,800.

3. Trout ate minnows. DDT was magnified 1.7 times, so the concentration of DDT in trout was 42,160 times greater than in the environment.

4. Gulls ate trout. DDT was magnified 4.8 times, so the concentration of DDT in gulls was over 200,000 times greater than in the environment.

DDT is especially harmful to large birds such as osprey and eagles. The chemical made the shells of the eggs of these large birds so thin that the eggs did not survive long enough to hatch.

Moving up the Food Chain

This diagram shows how DDT moved up a food chain in Long Island Sound. The color in each circle below represents a certain level of DDT.

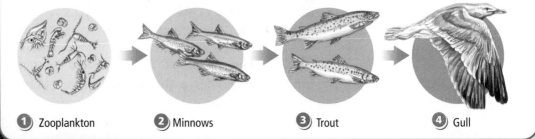

1. Zooplankton
2. Minnows
3. Trout
4. Gull

CHALLENGE Even though DDT was effective, some insects were not harmed by DDT. Predict what might happen to the numbers of those insects as a result of DDT use.

1.4

Biomes contain many ecosystems.

BEFORE, you learned

- Feeding relationships describe how energy flows through ecosystems
- The amount of available energy decreases as it flows through ecosystems

NOW, you will learn

- How biomes vary by region and by the plant life they support
- How different ecosystems make up a biome
- About the different land and water biomes on Earth

VOCABULARY

biome p. 30
coniferous p. 32
deciduous p. 33
estuary p. 36

THINK ABOUT

What do this plant's characteristics suggest about its environment?

A plant's overall shape and form help it to survive in its environment. Look closely at this plant in the photograph. Describe its shape. Does it have leaves? a stem? flowers? Look at the surrounding area. What do your observations suggest about the environment in general?

Regions of Earth are classified into biomes.

COMBINATION NOTES
Remember to take notes and draw a diagram for each of the six land biomes described in the text.

If you could travel along the 30° latitude line, either north or south of the equator, you'd notice an interesting pattern. You would see deserts give way to grasslands and grasslands give way to forests. Across Earth, there are large geographic areas that are similar in climate and that have similar types of plants and animals. Each of these regions is classified as a **biome** (BY-OHM). There are six major land biomes on Earth, as shown on the map on page 31.

Climate is an important factor in land biomes. Climate describes the long-term weather patterns of a region, such as average yearly rainfall and temperature ranges. Climate also affects soil type. Available water, temperature, and soil are abiotic factors important in ecosystems. The fact that the abiotic factors of a particular biome are similar helps to explain why the ecosystems found in these biomes are similar. Biomes represent very large areas, which means that there will be many ecosystems within a biome.

Each land biome is characterized by a particular climate, the quality of the soil, and the plant life found there.

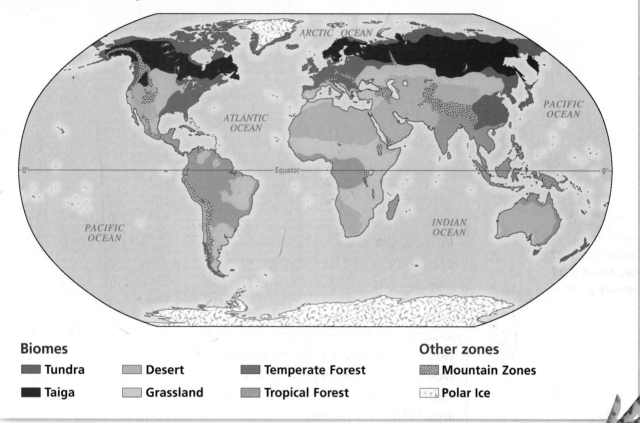

Biomes

- Tundra
- Taiga
- Desert
- Grassland
- Temperate Forest
- Tropical Forest

Other zones

- Mountain Zones
- Polar Ice

Taiga and Tundra

If you go to the northernmost regions of Earth, you will find two biomes—tundra and taiga—that are characterized by long cold winters and short cool summers. In the Arctic tundra, temperatures can go as low as –50°C, with a high of about 18°C. Temperature ranges in the taiga (TY-guh) are similar, –40°C to 20°C.

The tundra doesn't get much precipitation, less than 25 centimeters each year. Yet the area is wet because cold temperatures keep the water from evaporating. One of the important characteristics of tundra is permafrost, a deep layer of permanently frozen soil that lies just below the surface soil. Permafrost prevents trees from taking root in the tundra. Plants of the tundra are small and include mosses, grasses, and woody shrubs. Organisms called lichens also do well in the tundra.

The producers of tundra ecosystems support rodents, caribou, and musk oxen. Grizzly bears, white fox, and snowy owls are predators found there. Migrating birds come to nest in the tundra, feeding on insects that mature in summer.

snowy owl

Tundra Only small plants and lichens grow in the tundra because the soil below the surface is frozen.

Taiga Evergreen trees grow in the taiga, where the ground is cold but not frozen.

Even though the temperatures of the taiga are similar to those of the tundra, the taiga has more precipitation, 30 to 60 centimeters a year. The effect of this is that there is more snow on the ground, which insulates the soil below, keeping it from permanently freezing.

Taiga ecosystems are characterized by evergreen trees called **coniferous** (koh-NIHF-uhr-uhs) trees. These trees have needlelike leaves that produce food all year long. This is an advantage in taiga ecosystems because decomposers work slowly in the cold, so the soil is low in nutrients. The wood and leaves of these trees feed insects and their seeds feed birds and squirrels. Taiga ecosystems support deer, elk, snowshoe hares, and beavers. Predators include lynx, owls, bears, and wolves.

Desert and Grassland

collared lizard

Deserts and grasslands are biomes found toward the middle latitudes. You can see from the map on page 31 that a desert biome often leads into a grassland biome. What deserts and grasslands have in common is that they do not get enough precipitation to support trees.

Some deserts are cold and some deserts are hot, but all deserts are characterized by their dry soil. Less than 25 centimeters of rain falls each year in a desert. Desert plants, like the cactus, and desert animals, like the collared lizard, can get by on very little water. Small burrowing animals like the kangaroo rat and ground squirrel are part of desert ecosystems. Desert predators include snakes, owls, and foxes.

Grassland ecosystems develop in areas of moderate rainfall, generally from 50 to 90 centimeters each year. There is enough rain to support grasses, but too little rain to support forests. Periodic wildfires and droughts keep smaller shrubs and tree seedlings from growing. Summers in grassland ecosystems are warm, up to 30°C, but winters are cold.

Grasses do well in large open areas. The more rain a grassland ecosystem gets, the higher the grasses grow. These ecosystems support seed-eating rodents that make their burrows in the grassland soil. There are also large grazing animals, like bison, wild horses, gazelle, and zebra. Predators include wolves, tigers, and lions.

Desert Plants of the desert are adapted to survive in dry soil. Many must also survive high daytime temperatures.

Grassland Grasslands receive enough rain to support grasses. Wildfires keep shrubs and trees from growing.

Temperate Forest and Tropical Forest

Trees need more water than smaller plants, shrubs, and grasses. So forest biomes are usually located in regions where more water is available. The taiga is a forest biome. There the coniferous trees survive on smaller amounts of precipitation because the cold weather limits evaporation. Across the middle latitudes, temperate forests grow where winters are short and 75 to 150 centimeters of precipitation fall each year. Near the equator, there are no winters. There, tropical forests grow where 200 to 450 centimeters of rain fall each year.

Most temperate forests are made up of deciduous trees, sometimes referred to as broadleaf trees. **Deciduous** (dih-SIHJ-oo-uhs) trees drop their leaves as winter approaches and then grow new leaves in spring.

Temperate Forest
Temperate forests contain many trees with leaves that change color and fall as winter approaches.

Tropical Forest
Tropical forests are warm enough that trees stay green during the entire year.

The most common broadleaf trees in North American deciduous forests are oak, birch, beech, and maple. Temperate forests support a wide variety of animals. Animals like mice, chipmunks, squirrels, raccoons, and deer live off seeds, fruit, and insects. Predators include wolves, bobcats, foxes, and mountain lions.

Most temperate forests in North America are deciduous. However, the wet winters and dry summers in the Pacific Northwest support forests made up mostly of coniferous trees—redwoods, spruce, and fir. These forests are referred to as temperate rain forests. The largest trees in the United States are found in these temperate rain forests.

Tropical forests are located near the equator, where the weather is warm all year, around 25°C. The tropical rain forest is the wettest land biome, with a rainfall of 250 to 400 centimeters each year. The trees tend to have leaves year round. This provides an advantage because the soil is poor in nutrients. High temperatures cause materials to break down quickly, but there are so many plants the nutrients get used up just as quickly.

More types of animals, plants, and other organisms live in the tropical rain forest than anywhere else on Earth. The trees grow close together and support many tree-dwelling animals like monkeys, birds, insects, and snakes. There are even plants, like orchids and vines, that grow on top of the trees.

 CHECK YOUR READING How does the variety of plants in a biome affect the variety of animals in a biome?

How can you graph climate data for your area?

PROCEDURE

1. Gather local data on the average monthly precipitation and the average monthly temperature for a 12-month period.

2. On graph paper, mark off 12 months along the *x*-axis. Make a *y*-axis for each side of the graph, marking one "Temperature (°C)" and the other "Precipitation (mm)."

3. Plot the average precipitation for each month as a bar graph.

4. Plot the average temperature for each month as a line graph.

WHAT DO YOU THINK?

- How much precipitation did the area receive overall?
- What is the temperature range for the area?

CHALLENGE Collect data for the same location, going back 10, 20, and 30 years ago. Graph the data for each of these and compare these graphs to your original graph. Has the climate in your area changed? How might severe changes in climate affect the plant and animal life in your area?

SKILL FOCUS
Graphing data

MATERIALS
- graph data
- 2 colored pencils

TIME
20 minutes

Water covers most of Earth's surface.

Close to three-quarters of Earth's surface is covered by water. Water, or aquatic, biomes can be divided into two broad categories: freshwater biomes and saltwater biomes. Plants have a role as producers in the water biomes that are closely surrounded by land—in ponds and streams and wetlands, and in coastal areas. The food chains of deepwater ecosystems depend on tiny photosynthetic microorganisms called phytoplankton.

leopard frog

Freshwater Biomes

The ecosystems of freshwater biomes are affected by the qualities of the landscape in which they are found. For example, the running water of streams and rivers results from differences in elevation. In shallow rivers, green algae and plants grow in from the banks, providing food for insects and snails that feed fish, salamanders, turtles, and frogs. Plants in a freshwater biome, like a stream or river, may take root in the soil under the water if the water is not too deep or moving too fast. Phytoplankton are not part of river ecosystems because of the moving water.

Aquatic Biomes

Freshwater biomes include the still water of lakes, the running water of rivers, and estuaries where fresh and salt waters mix.

Lakes and Ponds

Estuaries

Rivers and Streams

Ponds and lakes have still water. Ponds are shallow and support many plants as producers. The deeper lakes depend much more on phytoplankton. Ponds and lakes support many different insects, shellfish, snakes, fish, and the land animals that feed off them.

 CHECK YOUR READING Name two types of freshwater biomes.

Estuaries are water ecosystems that mark a transition between freshwater and saltwater biomes. An **estuary** is the lower end of a river that feeds into the ocean, where fresh water and salt water mix. Marshes and wetlands are two types of estuaries. Estuaries are sometimes referred to as the nurseries of the sea because so many marine animals travel into the calm waters of an estuary to reproduce. Seaweed, marsh grasses, shellfish, and birds all thrive in estuaries.

Marine Biomes

Marine biomes are saltwater biomes. The three general marine biomes are coastal ocean, open ocean, and deep ocean. Beaches are part of the coastal ocean biome. Tidal pools also form along the coast as the tide comes in and goes out and the conditions constantly change. Organisms like crabs and clams are able to survive the ever-changing conditions to thrive in coastal areas.

Organisms in the open ocean receive less sunlight than in the coastal ocean, and the temperatures are colder. Many types of fish and

RESOURCE CENTER
CLASSZONE.COM
Find out more about land and aquatic biomes.

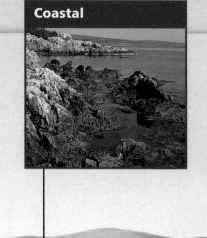

Coastal

Marine biomes include rocky and sandy shores as well as the open ocean and the deep waters below, where little or no light can reach.

Open Ocean

Deep Ocean

other marine animals and floating seaweed live in the upper ocean. There are no plants in the open ocean. The producers at the bottom of the food chain are different types of phytoplankton.

The deep-ocean regions are much colder and darker than the upper ocean. In the deep ocean there is no sunlight available for photosynthesis. The animals in the deep ocean either feed on each other or on material that falls down from upper levels of the ocean. Many organisms in deep ocean biomes can only be seen with a microscope.

1.4 Review

KEY CONCEPTS

1. In biomes located on land, abiotic factors are used to classify the different biome types. What are these abiotic factors?

2. Name a characteristic type of plant for each of the six land biomes.

3. Name six different aquatic biomes.

CRITICAL THINKING

4. **Predict** If an ecosystem in the grassland biome started to receive less and less rainfall every year, what new biome would be established?

5. **Infer** Name some abiotic factors that affect aquatic biomes and ecosystems.

⬥ **CHALLENGE**

6. **Apply** Use the map on page 31 to list the following four biomes in the order you would find them moving from the equator to the poles.

   • desert
   • taiga
   • tropical Forest
   • tundra

the BIG idea

Matter and energy together support life within an environment.

CONTENT REVIEW
CLASSZONE.COM

◀ KEY CONCEPTS SUMMARY

1.1 Ecosystems support life.

Ecosystems are made up of living things (biotic) and nonliving things (abiotic).

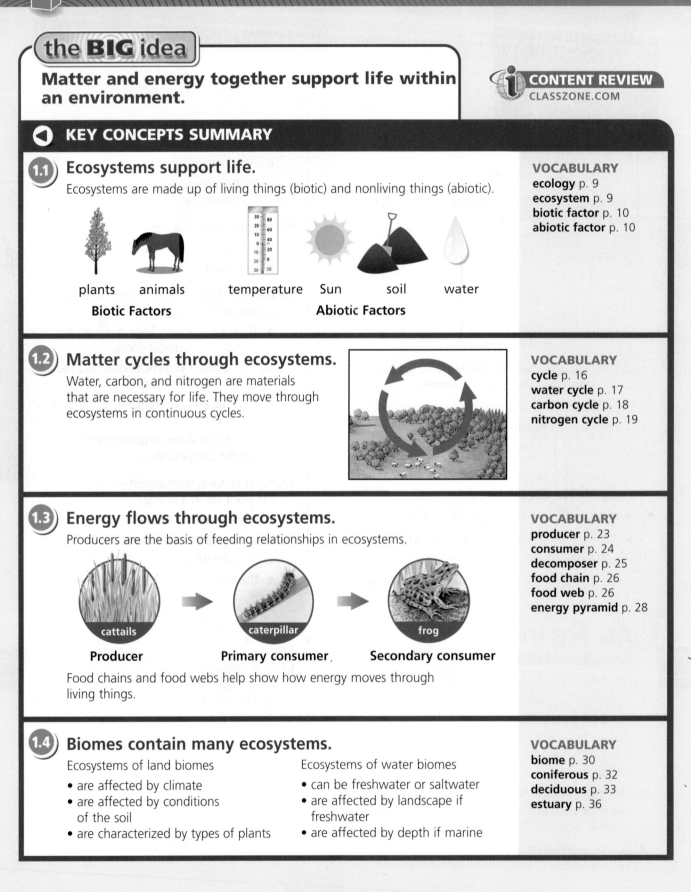

plants   animals

Biotic Factors

temperature   Sun   soil   water

Abiotic Factors

VOCABULARY
ecology p. 9
ecosystem p. 9
biotic factor p. 10
abiotic factor p. 10

1.2 Matter cycles through ecosystems.

Water, carbon, and nitrogen are materials that are necessary for life. They move through ecosystems in continuous cycles.

VOCABULARY
cycle p. 16
water cycle p. 17
carbon cycle p. 18
nitrogen cycle p. 19

1.3 Energy flows through ecosystems.

Producers are the basis of feeding relationships in ecosystems.

cattails

caterpillar

frog

Producer   **Primary consumer**   **Secondary consumer**

Food chains and food webs help show how energy moves through living things.

VOCABULARY
producer p. 23
consumer p. 24
decomposer p. 25
food chain p. 26
food web p. 26
energy pyramid p. 28

1.4 Biomes contain many ecosystems.

Ecosystems of land biomes
- are affected by climate
- are affected by conditions of the soil
- are characterized by types of plants

Ecosystems of water biomes
- can be freshwater or saltwater
- are affected by landscape if freshwater
- are affected by depth if marine

VOCABULARY
biome p. 30
coniferous p. 32
deciduous p. 33
estuary p. 36

Write a statement describing how the terms in each pair are similar and different.

1. biotic, abiotic

2. producer, consumer

3. food chain, food web

The table shows the meanings of word roots that are used in many science terms.

Root	Meaning
bio-	life
ecos-	house
-ogy	study of

Use the information in the table to write definitions for the following terms.

4. ecology

5. biome

6. ecosystem

Reviewing Key Concepts

Multiple Choice *Choose the letter of the best answer.*

7. Which best describes the components of an ecosystem?
   a. light, water, soil, and temperature
   b. autotrophs and heterotrophs
   c. biotic and abiotic factors
   d. producers, consumers, and decomposers

8. What is the primary source of energy for most ecosystems?
   a. water   c. soil
   b. nitrogen   d. sunlight

9. What is the process by which the water in rivers, lakes, and oceans is converted to a gas and moves into the atmosphere?
   a. precipitation   c. condensation
   b. evaporation   d. transpiration

10. The process called nitrogen fixation is essential for life on Earth. Which of the following is an example of nitrogen fixation?
    a. Plants take in nitrogen gas from the atmosphere.
    b. Animals take in nitrogen gas from the atmosphere.
    c. Water absorbs nitrogen.
    d. Bacteria convert nitrogen gas into a form that plants can use.

11. Which organism is a decomposer?
    a. vulture   c. musk ox
    b. sunflower   d. fungus

12. How are decomposers important in an ecosystem?
    a. They make atmospheric nitrogen available to plants in a usable form.
    b. They convert organic matter into more complex compounds.
    c. They are an important source of food for scavengers.
    d. They break down organic matter into simpler compounds.

13. What factor is least important in determining the plant life in a biome?
    a. average annual rainfall
    b. average annual temperature
    c. the type of soil
    d. the type of animals living there

Short Answer *Write a short answer to each question.*

14. Write a paragraph to describe how carbon dioxide gas in the atmosphere can become part of the carbon compounds found inside animals.

15. Write a paragraph to explain how the amount of available energy changes as you move from producers to consumers in a food web.

16. Write a paragraph to describe one important way in which the flow of energy through ecosystems is different from the cycling of matter.

Use the diagram to answer the next four questions.

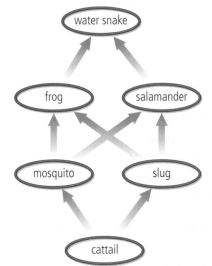

17. **CONNECT** What does the diagram above represent and how does it relate to energy in an ecosystem?

18. **CLASSIFY** Identify each of the animals in the diagram above as a producer, primary consumer, or secondary consumer or tertiary consumer.

19. **APPLY** Another animal that is found in many wetlands ecosystems is the shrew. The shrew eats salamanders and slugs and is eaten by water snakes. Copy the diagram above and show how you would add the shrew to the diagram.

20. **CONNECT** Use the diagram above to make an energy pyramid. If only one-tenth of the energy available at each level is passed on to the next higher level, how much of the energy in a cattail is transferred to a salamander?

21. **SYNTHESIZE** Why would it be difficult to show a decomposer as part of an energy pyramid?

22. **RANK** Arrange the following list of biomes according to the relative amounts of precipitation in each, going from the least amount to the most: grassland, desert, deciduous forest, taiga, tropical rain forest.

23. **SYNTHESIZE** Why are plants but not animals considered an important factor in classifying a land biome?

24. **SUMMARIZE** Draw a diagram that illustrates aquatic biomes. On your diagram label the following: freshwater river, freshwater lake, estuary, coastal zone, open ocean zone. How do abiotic factors differ among these biomes?

25. **COMPARE AND CONTRAST** In what ways is your home like an ecosystem? In what ways is it different?

26. **APPLY** Describe a change in an abiotic factor that affected living factors in an ecosystem near you.

the BIG idea

27. **CLASSIFY** Look again at the photograph on pages 6–7. Now that you have finished the chapter, how would you change or add details to your answer to the question on the photograph?

28. **SYNTHESIZE** Write one or more paragraphs describing how matter and energy together support life in an ecosystem. You may use examples from one specific ecosystem if you wish. In your description, use each of the following terms. Underline each term in your answer.

ecosystem	decomposer
food web	nitrogen cycle
producer	carbon cycle
primary consumer	secondary consumer

UNIT PROJECTS

If you are doing a unit project, make a folder for your project. Include in your folder a list of the resources you will need, the date on which the project is due, and a schedule to track your progress. Begin gathering data.

Interpreting Graphs

Choose the letter of the best response.

The graphs below show average monthly temperature and precipitation for one year in Staunton, Virginia, an area located in a temperate deciduous forest biome.

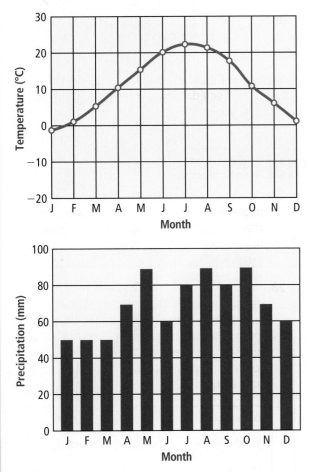

SOURCE: NASA

1. What was the average temperature during July?
   a. 20°
   b. 10°
   c. 23°
   d. 0°

2. Which months had the most precipitation?
   a. January, February, March
   b. May, August, October
   c. July, August, September
   d. December, January, February

3. What were conditions during May?
   a. warm and moist
   b. warm and dry
   c. cool and moist
   d. cool and dry

4. Which temperature is closest to the average temperature for the year shown?
   a. about 16°
   b. about 0°
   c. about 20°
   d. about 10°

5. How much precipitation would you estimate fell as snow in the year shown?
   a. less than 50 mm
   b. between 50 and 100 mm
   c. between 100 and 200 mm
   d. over 200 mm

Extended Response

6. Most of the United States is part of a temperate deciduous forest biome. The deciduous forest biome has four seasons. Trees in this biome lose their leaves yearly. Use this information, as well as the information in the graphs, to describe the seasons in the temperate deciduous forest biome.

7. Write a paragraph in which you describe a typical ecosystem in your city or town. In your answer include biotic factors such as plants, animals, and other organisms. Also include abiotic factors such as light, temperature, soil, and water. Finish your description by saying how you and other humans affect the ecosystem.

Interactions Within Ecosystems

the BIG idea

Living things within an ecosystem interact with each other and the environment.

How do living things interact?

Key Concepts

SECTION

2.1 Groups of living things interact within ecosystems.
Learn about how different organisms share living areas, interact in larger communities, and show different patterns within those communities.

SECTION

2.2 Organisms can interact in different ways.
Learn about the different types of interactions in an ecosystem, including competition, cooperation, and symbiosis.

SECTION

2.3 Ecosystems are always changing.
Learn about the limits and boundaries of organisms within an ecosystem and how ecosystems may change over time.

Internet Preview

CLASSZONE.COM

Chapter 2 online resources: Content Review, Simulation, two Resource Centers, Math Tutorial, Test Practice

EXPLORE (the BIG idea)

How Do Living Things Interact Where You Live?

Take your notebook outside. Observe how different living things interact. Record your observations.

Observe and Think Do the interactions you see benefit both living things or just one? Do they involve just animals or plants and animals?

How Many Roles Can a Living Thing Have in an Ecosystem?

While you are outside, choose an organism within your view and think about how it fits into the ecosystem.

Observe and Think In what way does the organism fit into feeding relationships in the ecosystem? What are some other roles the organism plays?

Internet Activity: Carrying Capacity

Go to **ClassZone.com** to simulate the carrying capacity of an area for a population of deer.

Observe and Think What factors other than available food might affect the carrying capacity for a popuation of deer?

NSTA
scilinks.org
SCILINKS

Populations and Communities **Code: MDL002**

Getting Ready to Learn

◀ CONCEPT REVIEW

- Ecosystems support life.
- Different ecosystems make up a biome.

◀ VOCABULARY REVIEW

producer p. 23   **food chain** p. 26

consumer p. 24   **food web** p. 26

interaction *See Glossary.*

CONTENT REVIEW
CLASSZONE.COM

Review concepts and vocabulary.

▶ TAKING NOTES

OUTLINE

As you read, copy the headings on your paper in the form of an outline. Then add notes in your own words that summarize what you read.

VOCABULARY STRATEGY

Write each new vocabulary term in the center of a **four square** diagram. Write notes in the squares around each term. Include definition, some characteristics, and some examples of the term. If possible, write some things that are not examples of the terms.

See the Note-Taking Handbook on pages R45–R51.

SCIENCE NOTEBOOK

I. Groups of living things interact within ecosystems.

  A. Organisms occupy specific living areas.

    1. populations: same species in one area

    2. habitat and niche: place where organisms live; role of organisms

    3. community: several populations living together

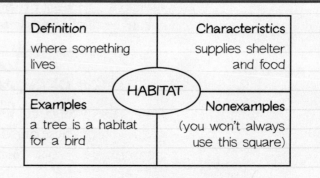

Definition	Characteristics
where something lives	supplies shelter and food
HABITAT	
Examples	Nonexamples
a tree is a habitat for a bird	(you won't always use this square)

2.1

Groups of living things interact within ecosystems.

◀ **BEFORE, you learned**

- Abiotic and biotic factors interact in an ecosystem
- Matter and energy necessary for life move through the environment

▶ **NOW, you will learn**

- How groups of organisms interact in an ecosystem
- About levels of organization in an ecosystem
- About living patterns of different groups of organisms

VOCABULARY

species p. 45
population p. 46
habitat p. 46
niche p. 47
community p. 48

EXPLORE Counting Animals

How can you use a grid to estimate the number of animals in an area?

PROCEDURE

① Mark off an area on the graph paper as shown. Count the number of large squares in that area.

② Use a handful of rice to represent a group of animals. Spread the rice evenly within the area you marked. Count the number of "animals" inside one large square.

③ Use a calculator to multiply the counts from steps 1 and 2. This will give you an estimate of the total number of "animals." Check your answer by counting all the grains of rice.

WHAT DO YOU THINK?
- How close was your estimate to the actual number?
- What would prevent a scientist from making an actual count of animals in an area?

MATERIALS
- handful of rice
- large-grid graph paper
- marker
- calculator

Organisms occupy specific living areas.

On a walk through the woods, you may see many different plants and animals. These organisms, like all living things, depend on their environment to meet their needs. The particular types of living things you see will depend on the characteristics of the area you are visiting.

Scientists group living things according to their shared characteristics. The smallest grouping is the species. Scientists consider organisms to be members of the same **species** (SPEE-sheez) if the organisms are so similar that they can produce offspring that can also produce offspring. Members of a species can successfully reproduce.

READING TiP

The terms *species*, *specific*, and *special* come from the same Latin root meaning "kind." A species is a kind, or type, of organism.

Galápagos Island Populations

A population is a group of the same organisms that live in the same area.

Cacti

Crabs

Iguanas

Populations

Scientists use the term **population** to mean a group of organisms of the same species that live in a particular area. In a way, this is similar to the population of people who live in a particular city or town. You can then think of those people who live in different cities or towns as belonging to different populations. It is the boundary of an area that defines a population. In the study of ecology, members of the same species that live in different areas belong to different populations.

A biological population can be a group of animals or a group of plants. It can be a group of bacteria or fungi or any other living thing. Populations of many different species will be found living in the same area. For example, the photographs above show different populations of organisms that all live in the same place—on one of the Galápagos Islands. The island has a population of cacti, a population of crabs, and a population of iguanas.

 CHECK YOUR READING What is the difference between a species and a population?

Habitats and Niches

The Galápagos Islands are a small group of volcanic islands, off the coast of South America, that are famous for their unusual plant and animal life. These islands are the **habitat**—the physical location—where these plants and animals live. Island habitats have certain physical characteristics that describe them, including the amount of precipitation, a range of temperatures, and the quality of the soil. Different habitats have different characteristics.

Galápagos Island Habitat

This island habitat is home to many different populations.

Galápagos Islands

cacti

crabs

iguanas

READING VISUALS What resources are available in this habitat?

A habitat is filled with different species, each of which depends on the habitat's resources to meet its needs. The characteristics of a habitat determine the species of plants that can grow there. The species of plants found in a habitat, in turn, determine the species of animals and other organisms that will do well there.

Different populations within a habitat interact. They are part of the flow of energy and matter through an ecosystem. For example, in the Galápagos Island scene above, the cacti capture the Sun's energy and store fresh water. They also provide food for the iguana, who eats the cactus leaves. The cactus is a producer and the iguana is a primary consumer. The crabs of the Galápagos are secondary consumers that feed on other shellfish. Each of these organisms has a role to play in the habitat, a role which is referred to as its **niche** (nihch).

The niche an organism fills in a habitat is not limited to its place in a food web. Plants provide nesting sites as well as food. The droppings left behind by animals fertilize soil and often spread seed. Generally, no two species will fill exactly the same niche in a habitat.

Communities

Take a mental tour of your school. Note that you share space with people who do many different things—students, teachers, custodians, librarians, counselors, and many others. They all work together and help each other. We often say that a school is a community.

Scientists use the term *community* in a slightly different way. A biological **community** is a group of populations that live in a particular area and interact with one another. Cacti, iguanas, and crabs are part of the Galápagos Island community. This community also includes populations of tortoises, finches, fleas, bacteria, and many other species.

 CHECK YOUR READING How is a school community similar to a community of living things?

The environment can be organized into five levels.

OUTLINE
Add the different levels of the environment to your outline. Make sure to explain each term in the supporting details.

The five terms—biome, ecosystem, community, population, and organism—describe the environment at different levels.

1. **Biome** A biome describes in very general terms the climate and types of plants that are found in similar places around the world.

2. **Ecosystem** Within each biome are many ecosystems. Inside an ecosystem, living and nonliving factors interact to form a stable system. An ecosystem is smaller than a biome and includes only organisms and their local environment.

3. **Community** A community is made up of the living components of the ecosystem. In a community, different plants, animals, and other organisms interact with each other.

4. **Population** A population is a group of organisms of the same species that live in the same area.

5. **Organism** An organism is a single individual animal, plant, fungus, or other living thing. As the picture on page 49 shows, an organism plays a part in each level of the environment.

Patterns exist in populations.

Members of a population settle themselves into the available living space in different ways, forming a pattern. Populations may be crowded together, be spread far apart, or live in small groups. A population may also show a pattern over time. The number of individuals in the population may rise and fall, depending on the season or other conditions, or as a result of interactions with other organisms.

Levels in the Environment

Organisms living in an African savannah illustrate the different levels of the environment.

Grassland

Equator

1 Biome
The African savannah is part of a grassland biome.

2 Ecosystem
The community of organisms, along with water, soil, and other abiotic factors, make up an ecosystem.

3 Community
Populations of wildebeests, gazelles, lions, and grasses share the same living areas and resources. These and other populations form a savannah community.

4 Population
Gazelles travel together in herds looking for areas to graze in. The total number of gazelles in an ecosystem is called a population of gazelles.

5 Organism
The gazelle lives in various grassland habitats in eastern Africa and fills a particular niche.

READING VISUALS Describe the gazelle's place in each level of the environment.

Patterns in Living Space

The patterns formed by a population often show how the population meets its needs. For example, in California's Mojave desert the pale soil is dotted with dark-green shrubs called creosote bushes. A surprising thing about the bushes is their even spacing. No human shaped this habitat, however. The bushes are the same distance from each other because the roots of each bush release a toxin, a type of poison, that prevents the roots of other bushes from growing.

The distribution of animals in a habitat is often influenced by how they meet their needs. Animals must be able to reach their food supply and have places to raise their young. If you put up bird houses for bluebirds on your property, they must be spaced at least a hundred meters apart. Bluebirds need a large area of their own around their nest in order to collect enough insects to feed their young.

READING TIP

As you read this paragraph, note the pattern of wilde-beests and elephants in the photograph.

Sometimes, the particular pattern of individuals in a living space helps a population survive. Herring swim in schools, with the individual fish spaced close together. Wildebeests roam African grasslands in closely packed herds. These animals rely on the group for their safety. Even if one member of the group is attacked, many more will survive.

 CHECK YOUR READING What are some reasons for the spacing patterns observed in different populations?

READING VISUALS COMPARE AND CONTRAST How would you describe the spacing of these elephants and wildebeests?

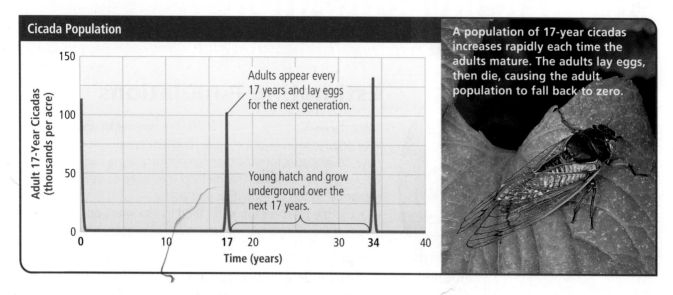

Cicada Population

Adult 17-Year Cicadas (thousands per acre)

Adults appear every 17 years and lay eggs for the next generation.

Young hatch and grow underground over the next 17 years.

Time (years)

A population of 17-year cicadas increases rapidly each time the adults mature. The adults lay eggs, then die, causing the adult population to fall back to zero.

Patterns in Time

At a spring picnic, you would rarely see the wasps called yellow jackets. At a fall picnic, however, they swarm to the food. This is an example of a population whose size changes with time. In spring, the queen wasp lays eggs and new wasps hatch. She continues to lay eggs all summer and the population grows. When winter comes, all the wasps except the queen die, and the population decreases.

Many birds that nest in North America in summer fly south to Central and South America in winter. There they find enough food and good nesting sites. In North America, this seasonal pattern leads to small bird populations in winter and large ones in summer.

The graph above shows an unusual pattern of population growth. Certain species of cicadas appear only every 17 years. Because no other species can rely on these insects as their main source of food, the cicadas survive long enough to lay eggs when they do appear.

2.1 Review

KEY CONCEPTS

1. What are two characteristics of a population?

2. Order these terms from the simplest to the most complex: biome, community, ecosystem, organism, population.

3. How do the terms *habitat* and *niche* relate to each other?

CRITICAL THINKING

4. **Apply** Choose a biological community in your region. Describe some of the populations that make up that community.

5. **Infer** How might the seasonal patterns of insect populations relate to the seasonal patterns of bird populations?

⚠ CHALLENGE

6. **Apply** The Explore activity on page 45 shows one way in which scientists sample a population to determine its total size. Would this method work for estimating the size of a population of 17-year cicadas? Why or why not?

CHAPTER INVESTIGATION

Estimating Populations

OVERVIEW AND PURPOSE The number of animals in a wild population cannot be easily counted. Wildlife biologists have developed a formula that can estimate a population's size by using small samples. This method is referred to as mark and recapture. In this investigation you will
- use the mark-recapture method to estimate population size
- test the effectiveness of the mark-recapture method by simulating an outbreak of disease in a population

▶ Problem

How effective is the mark-recapture method in estimating population size?

▶ Hypothesize

Write a hypothesis to explain how you will use a sudden change in population size to determine the effectiveness of the mark-recapture method. Your hypothesis should take the form of an "If . . . , then . . . , because . . ." statement.

MATERIALS
- paper bag
- white kidney beans
- 2 colored markers
- calculator

▶ Procedure

1. Make two data tables in your **Science Notebook,** like the ones shown on page 53.

2. From your teacher, obtain a paper bag containing a "population" of white kidney beans.

   step 3

3. Remove a small handful of beans. Count the sample and record the count in Table 1, under First Capture Total.

4. Use a colored marker to mark your sample population. Return the beans to the bag, and gently shake the bag to mix all the beans.

5. Remove and count a second sample of beans. Record the count in Table 1, under Recapture Total.

6. Count the number of beans from this sample that were marked from the first capture. Record this number in Table 1, under Recapture Marked. Return all the beans to the bag.

7 Use a calculator and the following formula to estimate the population size. Record the estimate in Table 1 as the Calculated Population Estimate.

$$\frac{\text{First Capture Total} \times \text{Recapture Total}}{\text{Recapture Marked}} = \text{Population Estimate}$$

8 Disease strikes. Remove a small handful of beans from the bag. Count the beans, and record this count in Table 2, under Killed by Disease. Set these beans aside.

9 Repeat steps 3–7 to mark and recapture your survivor population. This time use a different colored marker to mark your sample population, and only include the beans marked in the second color in your counts.

10 Fill in Data Table 2 for the survivor population. Use the formula from step 7 to calculate your estimate of the survivor population.

11 Once you have calculated your estimate of survivors, dump out the paper bag and count all the beans that were inside. Record this count in Table 2, under Actual Survivors Total.

▶ Observe and Analyze
Write It Up

1. CALCULATE From Table 2 add together the number of actual survivors and the number killed by disease. Put this in Table 1, under Actual Population Total.

2. CALCULATE Find the percentage of the population affected by disease using the following formula:

$$\frac{\text{Killed by disease} \times 100}{\text{Actual Population Total}} = \text{Percentage affected}$$

▶ Conclude
Write It Up

1. INFER How did the estimated number of beans compare with the actual number?

2. IDENTIFY LIMITS What aspects of this investigation most likely would not be possible in a natural habitat? Why not?

3. EVALUATE Compare your results with your hypothesis. Do your data support your hypothesis?

▶ INVESTIGATE Further

CHALLENGE Determine if using larger samples of a population gives better population estimates. Get another bag of unmarked beans from your teacher. Use a spreadsheet program, if available, to record your data and calculate the results.

Estimating Populations
Table 1. Population sampling before disease

First Capture Total	Recapture Total	Recapture Marked	Calculated Population Estimate	Actual Population Total

Table 2. Population sampling after disease

Survivors First Capture Total	Survivors Recapture Total	Survivors Recapture Marked	Calculated Survivors Estimate	Killed by Disease	Actual Survivors Total

2.2 Organisms can interact in different ways.

◀ **BEFORE, you learned**

- Different populations live together in a habitat
- Different species fill different niches in a habitat
- There are patterns in the ways organisms interact with each other and their environment

▶ **NOW, you will learn**

- About different types of interactions in an ecosystem
- How some species benefit from interactions
- How some species are harmed by interactions

VOCABULARY

predator p. 55
prey p. 55
competition p. 55
cooperation p. 57
symbiosis p. 58
mutualism p. 58
commensalism p. 59
parasitism p. 59

THINK ABOUT

What are some of the ways people interact?

People in a community interact with each other in many ways. An interaction is the way a person behaves toward or responds to another person. This photo-graph shows groups of people at a soccer game. There are players from two teams and fans who are watching the game. How would you describe the interactions among the people in this photograph?

Organisms interact in different ways.

The photograph above shows how members of a human community both compete and cooperate. Different members of the populations of a biological community also compete and cooperate. They not only share a habitat, but they also share the resources in that habitat. How different organisms interact depends on their relationship to each other.

A robin in a meadow finds a caterpillar and swallows it. This is one obvious way organisms in an ecosystem interact—one eats, and the other gets eaten. Organisms also compete. The robin may have to compete with a flicker to get the caterpillar. And organisms can coop-erate. Ants work together to build a nest, collect food, and defend their colony.

 CHECK YOUR READING Name three ways organisms may interact with each other in an ecosystem.

Predator and Prey

Many interactions between organisms in an ecosystem involve food. A food chain shows the feeding relationships between different species. There are producers and consumers. Another way to look at a food chain is through the interactions of predators and prey. The **predator** is an animal that eats another. The **prey** is an animal that is eaten by a predator. In a food chain, an organism can be both predator and prey. A meadowlark that feeds on a grasshopper is, in turn, eaten by a prairie falcon.

Predators can affect how members of their prey populations are distributed. Herring move together in a school and wildebeests travel in herds to protect themselves. It is the sick or older members of the population that will most likely be eaten by predators. Species of prey may also have adaptations that relate to the behavior of predators. This is true of cicadas and their long reproductive cycles.

Prey populations, in turn, affect the location and number of predator populations. For example some birds are predators feeding on insects. One factor that may affect movement of birds from one location to another is the availability of insects.

▼ **REMINDER**

A *producer* is an organism that makes its own food; a *consumer* is an organism that eats another organism for food.

Competition

In a team game, two teams compete against each other with the same goal in mind—to win the game. In a biological community, competition is for resources, not wins. **Competition** is the struggle between individuals or different populations for a limited resource.

In an ecosystem, competition may occur within the same species. Individual plants compete with each other for light, space, and nutrients. For example, creosote bushes compete with other creosote bushes for the same water supply. The toxins produced by the roots of one creosote bush prevent other creosote bushes from growing.

Competition also occurs between members of different species. In the tropical rain forests of Indonesia, vines called strangler figs compete with trees for water, light, and nutrients. The vine attaches itself to a host tree. As it grows, the vine surrounds and eventually kills the tree by blocking out sunlight and using up available water and nutrients.

INFER Do you think a strangler fig could survive on its own?

host tree

strangler fig

Competition

Competition between species
Two different species, hyenas and vultures, compete for the remains of a dead animal.

Competition within species Two male deer lock horns as they battle over territory.

Competition occurs between species and within species. For example, vultures and hyenas will compete over the food left in the remains of a dead animal. Wolves will compete with one another over territory. A wolf will mark its territory by urinating on trees and so warn off other wolves. Animals also compete over territory by fighting, using threatening sounds, and putting on aggressive displays.

Competition within species often occurs during the mating season. Male birds use mating songs and displays of feathers to compete for the attention of females. Male hippopotamuses fight to attract female hippopotamuses. Male crickets chirp to attract female crickets.

 CHECK YOUR READING What sorts of resources do plants and animals compete for?

READING TiP

Compare and contrast the meanings of *competition* and *coexistence*.

Competition does not occur between all populations that share the same resources. Many populations can coexist in a habitat—different species can live together without causing harm to one another. Many different populations of plants coexist in a forest. Maple trees, beech trees, and birch trees can live side by side and still have enough water, nutrients, and sunlight to meet their needs.

INVESTIGATE Species Interactions

How do predator-prey populations interact?

Use these rules for predator-prey interaction for each round. If a predator card touches three or more prey cards, remove the prey cards touched. If the predator card does not touch at least three prey cards, remove the predator card and leave the prey cards. Predator cards are large, prey cards are small.

PROCEDURE

① Use masking tape to mark a boundary on a table top.

② Scatter five prey cards into the area. Take a predator card and toss it, trying to get it to land on the prey.

③ According to the rules above, remove the predators and prey that have "died." Record the number of predators and prey that have

"survived." This represents one generation.

④ Double the populations of predators and prey—they have "reproduced."

⑤ Scatter the prey cards into the area and then toss the predator cards as before. Repeat steps 3 and 4 for a total of 15 rounds (generations).

WHAT DO YOU THINK?

- How does the size of the prey population affect the predator population?
- How might the size of a habitat affect the interaction of predators and prey?

CHALLENGE Use graph paper and colored pencils to make a graph of your results. Or use a spreadsheet program if one is available to you.

SKILL FOCUS
Analyzing data

MATERIALS
- 20 10 × 10 cm cardboard squares— predators
- 200 3 × 3 cm paper squares— prey
- masking tape *for Challenge:*
- graph paper
- 2 colored pencils

TIME
30 minutes

predator

prey

Cooperation

Not all interactions in an ecosystem involve competition. **Cooperation** is an interaction in which organisms work in a way that benefits them all. Some predators cooperate when they hunt. Although individual lions may hunt on their own, they also hunt in packs to kill large prey.

Killer whales also cooperate when they hunt. The whales swim in packs called pods. The pod swims in circles around a school of fish, forcing the fish close together so they are easier to catch. Pod members may also take turns chasing a seal until it gets tired and is easily killed. The pod may even work together to attack larger species of whales.

Ants, bees, and termites are social insects. Members of a colony belong to different groups, called castes, and have different responsibilities. Some groups gather food while others defend the colony. Other animals, like apes and monkeys, live in family groups. Members of the family cooperate to care for their young.

Cooperation
Driver ants work together to bring food to their nest.

The survival of one species might depend on another species.

OUTLINE
Add a sentence about *symbiosis* to your outline and define the three types of symbiosis in the supporting details.

You have learned that many different organisms live together in a habitat. The fact that organisms live together forces them to interact in different ways. For example, an organism preys upon another for food. Or perhaps there is competition among organisms over resources such as food, water, and territory.

The actions of different organisms can be so closely related that the survival of one species depends on the action or presence of another. In such a relationship, at least one of the species is getting a resource that it needs to survive. Benefits of the relationship may include food, reproductive help, or protection.

The relationship between individuals of two different species who live together in a close relationship is called **symbiosis** (SIHM-bee-OH-sihs). This word means "living together." A symbiotic relationship may affect the partners in different ways.

- Both species benefit from the relationship.
- One species benefits while the other is not affected.
- One species benefits while the other is harmed.

Here are some examples for each of the three types of symbiosis.

Both Species Benefit

Mutualism The interaction between the hummingbird and the flower benefits both.

Stroll through a garden on a sunny day and notice the bees buzzing from flower to flower. Look closely at a single bee and you may see yellow pollen grains sticking to its hairy body. The relationship between the flower and the bee is an example of **mutualism** (MYOO-choo-uh-LIHZ-uhm)—an interaction between two species that benefits both. The bees get food in the form of nectar, and the flowers get pollen from other flowers, which they need to make seeds.

Many plants rely on mutualism to reproduce. The pollen needed to make seeds must be spread from flower to flower. The birds and insects that feed on the nectar in these flowers transfer pollen from one flower to the next. The seeds produced are then moved to new ground by animals that eat the seeds or the fruits that hold the seeds. This form of mutualism doesn't benefit the individual flower but instead ensures the survival of the species.

In some cases, mutualism is necessary for the survival of the organisms themselves. For example, termites are able to live off a food that most animals cannot digest: wood. The termites, in fact, can't digest wood either. However, they have living in their guts tiny single-celled organisms, protozoans, that can break the wood down into digestible components. The protozoans get a safe place to live, and the termites can take advantage of a plentiful food source.

RESOURCE CENTER
CLASSZONE.COM
Explore symbiotic relationships.

 CHECK YOUR READING Describe how a bee and a flower benefit from a symbiotic relationship.

One Species Benefits

Commensalism (kuh-MEHN-suh-LIHZ-uhm) is a relationship between two species in which one species benefits while the other is not affected. Orchids and mosses are plants that can have a commensal relationship with trees. The plants grow on the trunks or branches of trees. They get the light they need as well as nutrients that run down along the tree. As long as these plants do not grow too heavy, the tree is not affected.

Commensal relationships are very common in ocean ecosystems. Small fish called remoras use a type of built-in suction cup to stick to a shark's skin and hitch a ride. When the shark makes a kill, the remora eats the scraps. The shark makes no attempt to attack the remora. The remora benefits greatly from this commensal relationship; the shark is barely affected.

Not all commensal relationships involve food. Some fish protect themselves by swimming among the stinging tentacles of a moon jellyfish. The fish benefit from the relationship because the tentacles keep them safe from predators. The jellyfish is not helped or hurt by the presence of the fish. As in this example, it is common in commensal relationships for the species that benefits to be smaller than the species it partners with.

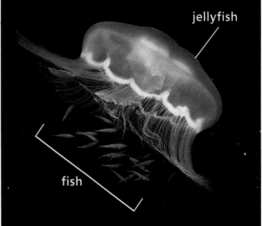

Commensalism The interaction between the jellyfish and the fish benefits the fish only.

One Species Is Harmed

There is one symbiotic relationship in which a small partner can harm a much larger host. **Parasitism** (PAR-uh-suh-TIHZ-uhm) is a relationship between two species in which one species benefits while the species it depends on, its host, is harmed. Parasites are often tiny organisms that feed off, and weaken, their hosts. Ticks, lice, and mites are external parasites that live on or attach to their host's skin. Other parasites, like tapeworms and ringworms, are internal parasites that live inside their hosts.

Symbiotic Relationships

Mutualism
Both species benefit from the relationship.

Commensalism
One species benefits while the other is not affected.

Parasitism
One species benefits while the other is harmed.

Parasitism
Mistletoe is a plant that takes nourishment from a tree, causing damage to the tree.

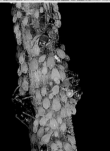

Mutualism
Aphids are insects that provide ants with a sweet liquid. Ants live alongside the aphids, protecting them from predators.

Commensalism
Lichens benefit from living on a tree, but the tree is not harmed.

Parasitism
Ticks are animals that attach to their hosts, feeding on the host's blood.

Mutualism
Nitrogen-fixing bacteria get their nourishment from the roots of certain plants, providing the plants with nitrogen in return.

Commensalism
Mice do well living near humans, living off the food scraps humans leave behind.

The relationship between cowbirds and warblers is an unusual type of association called nest or brood parasitism. Female cowbirds never build their own nests or rear their own young. Instead, they lay their eggs in warbler nests. Although nest parasitism does not harm the host warbler, it does harm the warbler species because either warblers eggs do not hatch, or the chicks do not survive. The warbler species is often harmed because cowbirds push most warbler eggs from the nest in order to make room for their own eggs. Once the cowbird chicks hatch, their larger size helps them to outcompete the smaller warbler chicks for food, so that the host's chicks starve.

host warbler

warbler chick   cowbird chick

Parasitism The larger cowbird chick is cared for by a warbler at the expense of the smaller warbler chick.

CHECK YOUR READING How is parasitism different from commensalism?

Interactions in an ecosystem are complex.

Different types of symbiosis occur throughout an ecosystem and often overlap. They may occur in the same locations, and the same species might be involved in more than one symbiotic relationship. The illustration on page 60 shows different symbiotic relationships that may occur in a backyard.

Symbiosis is just one of many interactions that take place in an ecosystem. The yard may have a garden, with individual tomato plants competing for water and nutrients; it may have ants cooperating to maintain a successful colony. An ecosystem is more than just a collection of biotic and abiotic factors. Interactions within an ecosystem help explain how resources are shared and used up and how energy flows through the system.

2.2 Review

KEY CONCEPTS

1. Name two ways in which members of the same species interact.

2. In what ways do members of different species interact?

3. Give an example of each type of symbiotic relationship: mutualism, commensalism, and parasitism.

CRITICAL THINKING

4. **Apply** Think of a biological community near you, and give an example of how one population has affected another.

5. **Compare and Contrast** Explain how symbiotic relationships are similar to and different from predator-prey interactions.

CHALLENGE

6. **Synthesize** Mutualism is more common in tropical ecosystems such as rain forests and coral reefs than in other ecosystems. Why do you think this is so?

Where Are the Salamanders?

At the Cottonwood Lake Study Area in rural Stutsman County, North Dakota, U.S. Fish and Wildlife Service biologists have been studying wetland ecosystems for more than 30 years. Salamanders are one of the most abundant species in these wetlands. But in May 2000, the researchers started noticing sick salamanders in one wetland. By July, most salamanders had died. What killed them?

▶ Observations

a. In the past, cold winter weather and food shortages have killed salamanders at Cottonwood Lake.

b. The sick salamanders had discolored skin and enlarged livers.

c. The previous year, leopard frogs in a nearby wetland were found dying from a contagious fungal infection.

d. A viral disease has killed tiger salamanders elsewhere in the West.

e. Both large, well-fed salamanders and small, poorly nourished salamanders died.

▶ Inferences

The following statements are possible inferences:

a. A food shortage caused salamanders to starve.

b. The fungal disease that killed leopard frogs also killed the salamanders

c. Salamanders were killed by a viral disease.

▶ Evaluate Inferences

On Your Own Which of the inferences are supported by the observations? Write the observations that support each of the inferences you identify.

As a Group Discuss your decisions. Come up with a list of reasonable inferences.

CHALLENGE What further observations would you make to test any of these inferences?

This barred tiger salamander can be found in many wetlands in the Great Plains.

2.3 Ecosystems are always changing.

D

◀ **BEFORE, you learned**

- Populations in an ecosystem interact in different ways
- Organisms can benefit from interactions in an ecosystem
- Organisms can be harmed by interactions in an ecosystem

▶ **NOW, you will learn**

- How different factors affect the size of a population
- How biological communities get established
- How biological communities change over time

VOCABULARY

limiting factor p. 64
carrying capacity p. 65
succession p. 66
pioneer species p. 66

EXPLORE Population Growth

How does sugar affect the growth of yeast?

PROCEDURE

1. Use a marker to label the cups A, B, C. Pour 150 mL of warm water into each cup. Mark the water level with the marker.
2. Add 1/2 teaspoon of dry yeast to each plastic cup and stir.
3. Add 1/4 teaspoon of sugar to cup B. Add 1 teaspoon of sugar to cup C. Stir.
4. Wait 15 minutes. Measure the height of the foam layer that forms in each cup.

WHAT DO YOU THINK?

- Which cup had the most foam, which cup had the least?
- Describe the effect of sugar on a population of yeast.

MATERIALS

- 3 clear plastic cups
- warm water
- sugar
- dry yeast
- measuring spoons
- measuring cup
- stirring rod
- marker
- ruler

Populations change over time.

REMINDER

A *population* is a group of organisms of the same species that live together in the same habitat.

You may have a strong memory of a park you visited as a little child. You remember collecting pine cones, listening to woodpeckers, and catching frogs. Then you visit again, years later, and the park has changed. Maybe more land has been added, there are more birds and trees. Or maybe the area around the park has been developed. There seem to be fewer woodpeckers, and you can't find any frogs. The community has changed. There are a lot of factors that affect the populations within a biological community. Some have to do with the organisms themselves. Others relate to the habitat.

Population Growth and Decline

One factor that obviously affects population size is how often organisms reproduce. Birth rate is a measure of the number of births in an animal population. It can also be a measure of the stability of an ecosystem. For example, black bears reproduce once every two years. If there is not enough food available, however, the female bear's reproductive cycle is delayed, and the bear population does not grow.

Predator-prey interactions also affect population size. The graphs show how an increase in the moose population—the prey—in Isle Royale National Park was followed by an increase in the island's population of wolves—the predators. The wolves preyed upon the moose, the moose population decreased, then the wolf population decreased.

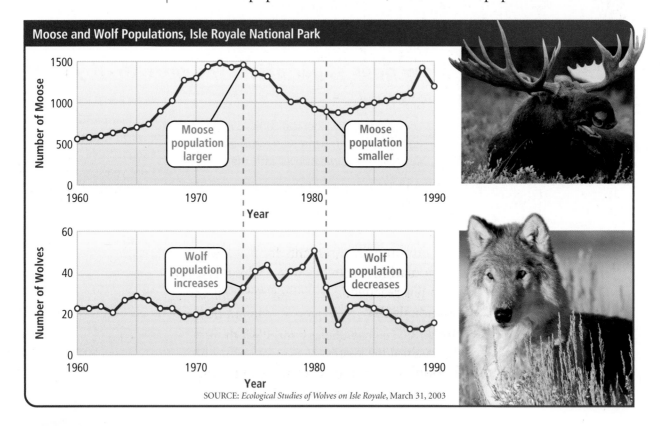

Moose and Wolf Populations, Isle Royale National Park

Moose population larger

Moose population smaller

Wolf population increases

Wolf population decreases

SOURCE: *Ecological Studies of Wolves on Isle Royale*, March 31, 2003

READING TiP

Note in the graphs above that it can take some time for the size of one population to affect the size of the other.

Any factor or condition that limits the growth of a population in an ecosystem is called a **limiting factor.** A large population of predators will limit the population of prey; a small population of prey will limit the population of predators. Too much or too little of any biotic or abiotic factor—like food, water, or light—makes an ecosystem unstable and brings about change.

A lack of nutrients in the soil is a limiting factor for plants. That is why farmers fertilize their crops. That same fertilizer, if it runs off into a lake, can increase the population of algae, another photosynthetic organism. A large population of algae can cover a lake with scum and use up oxygen needed by fish. This then limits the fish population.

What effect does spacing have upon a population of plants?

DESIGN —YOUR OWN— EXPERIMENT

Using the materials listed, design an experiment to test this hypothesis: "If plants grow too close together, the health of the population will be affected because the individual plants do not get enough of the nutrients and water that they need."

PROCEDURE

① Decide how to use the seeds, cups, and soil to test the hypothesis.

② Write up your experimental procedure. Include safety tips.

WHAT DO YOU THINK?

• What are the variables in your experiment?

• What evidence would you expect to see if your hypothesis is true?

CHALLENGE Conduct your experiment. Note that seeds must be planted near the top of the soil. A good measure for this is the tip of a pencil. Measure and record the growth of the seedlings. Allow the seedlings to grow for two weeks before drawing your conclusions.

SKILL FOCUS
Designing experiments

MATERIALS
• paper cups
• potting soil
• radish seeds
• water
• pencil
• ruler

TIME
20 minutes

Maintaining a Balance

Living things have certain minimum requirements for food, water, and living space. When a population reaches a state where it can no longer grow, the population has reached its **carrying capacity,** the maximum number of individuals that an ecosystem can support. You can see on page 64 that the graph for the moose population does appear to peak around 1500. Even if there were no wolves on the island of Isle Royale, the population of moose would still be limited because there is only so much food and space available.

 CHECK YOUR READING Explain the term *carrying capacity.*

VOCABULARY
Remember to make a four square diagram for *carrying capacity* in your notebook. Try to use *limiting factor* in your diagram.

An ecosystem's carrying capacity is different for each population. A meadow ecosystem will support many more bees and ants than bluebirds, for example. Isle Royale supports many more moose than wolves. The moose is a primary consumer of plants. It is at a lower level of the energy pyramid than the wolf, a secondary consumer.

Biotic factors can be limiting factors. These factors include the interactions between populations, such as competition, predation, and parasitism. Abiotic factors, such as temperature, availability of water or minerals, and exposure to wind, are also limiting.

Ecosystems change over time.

Take a walk in a New Hampshire woods and you may see the remains of old stone walls scattered about. A hundred years ago this land was mostly farmland. The farms were abandoned. And now, new trees have grown where farm animals once grazed.

Succession (suhk-SEHSH-uhn) is the gradual change in an ecosystem in which one biological community is replaced by another. The change from field to forest is an example of succession. Over time the grasses of open farmland are slowly replaced by small plants and shrubs, then trees.

Primary Succession

READING TiP

Succeed and *succession* come from the same Latin root word, *succedere*, meaning to go up or to follow after.

Very few places on Earth are without some form of life. Even when a lava flow covers an area or a glacier retreats and leaves behind an empty and barren environment, plants will move into the area and bring it back to life. These are examples of primary succession, the establishment of a new biological community.

Pioneer species are the first living things to move into a barren environment. In the illustration below, moss and lichen move in after a glacier retreats. There is little or no topsoil. Moss and lichen are common pioneers because they have tiny rootlike structures that can take hold on exposed rock.

Primary Succession

Primary succession can occur after a glacier retreats, when little topsoil is present.

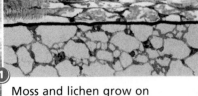

1 Moss and lichen grow on rock with little or no soil. These pioneer species break apart the surface rock.

2 Over time, the rock breaks down further, forming soil. Larger plants take root. These support populations of animals.

3 Coniferous trees take root in a deep layer of soil. A diversity of plants and animals are supported in this habitat.

As the pioneers grow, they gradually weaken the rock surface. The rock breaks down and weathers over time. Decaying plant matter adds nutrients, forming soil. Now a variety of small plants and shrubs can take root. These plants, in turn, support insects, birds, and small rodents. Eventually there is enough soil to support coniferous trees. Forests grow, providing a stable habitat for larger animals.

RESOURCE CENTER
CLASSZONE.COM

Learn more about succession.

Secondary Succession

Secondary succession takes place after a major disturbance to the biological community in a stable ecosystem. Despite the disturbance, the soil remains. A community can be disturbed by a natural event, like fire or flood, or it can be disturbed by human activity. A forest cleared or farmland abandoned can lead to secondary succession.

The illustration below shows secondary succession following a forest fire. The damage, as bad as it is, is surface damage. Below the surface, seeds and plant roots survive. After a time, grasses and small shrubs grow up among the decaying remains of the original plants. Birds, insects, and rodents return. Alder trees take root—alders are trees that put nutrients into the soil. Over time, a variety of trees and plants grow, providing food for a variety of animals.

CHECK YOUR READING What is the difference between primary and secondary succession?

Secondary Succession

Secondary succession occurs if soil remains after a disturbance, such as a forest fire.

① Plants at the surface are burned; however, below the surface seeds and some plant roots survive.

② Grasses and small shrubs sprout among the charred trees and vegetation. Smaller animals return.

③ Deciduous trees like elm and maple grow and mature. A forest habitat is reestablished. More animals are supported.

Patterns of Change

All types of ecosystems go through succession. Succession can establish a forest community, a wetland community, a coastal community, or even an ocean community. Succession can happen over tens or hundreds of years. The pattern is the same, however. First a community of producers is established. These are followed by decomposers and consumers, then more producers, then more decomposers and consumers. Over time, a stable biological community develops.

In a way, the establishment of a biological community is like planting a garden. You first prepare the soil. Perhaps you add compost. This adds organic matter and nutrients to the soil, which helps the soil hold water. With the right preparation, your vegetables and flowers should grow well.

Pioneer species can function in one of two ways in an ecological succession. They can help other species to grow or they can prevent species from getting established.

READING **TiP**

As you read about the two ways plant species function in succession, think in terms of cooperation and competition.

- Some plant species function a bit like gardeners. Trees such as alders have nitrogen-fixing bacteria on their roots that improve the nutrient content of the soil and allow other tree seedlings to grow. Pioneering species may also stabilize the soil, shade the soil surface, or add nutrients to the soil when they die and decay.

- Other plant species produce conditions that keep out other plants. The plants may release chemicals that keep other plants from taking root. Or a new species may outcompete other species by using up resources or better resisting a disease.

Such interactions between living things help to determine succession in an ecosystem.

2.3 Review

KEY CONCEPTS

1. Describe three factors that could limit the size of a population in a habitat.

2. List two natural disturbances and two human-made disturbances that can lead to succession.

3. What role do pioneer species play in succession?

CRITICAL THINKING

4. **Infer** How and why would secondary succession in a tundra habitat differ from secondary succession in a rainforest habitat?

5. **Predict** Suppose you are clearing an area in your yard to construct a small pond. Sketch the stages of succession that would follow this disturbance.

○ CHALLENGE

6. **Synthesize** Imagine you are the wildlife manager for a forest preserve that supports both moose and wolves. What types of information should you collect to determine the carrying capacity for each species?

Birth Rates and Populations

Ecologists pay careful attention to the yearly birth rates of endangered species. A birth rate is usually expressed as a fraction. It is the number of births divided by the number of adult females. A 2/5 birth rate for a population means that there are 2 births for every 5 adult females.

MATH TUTORIAL
CLASSZONE.COM

Click on Math Tutorial for more help with multiplying fractions and whole numbers.

Example

Suppose at a national park in Borneo, there is a 2/5 birth rate among orangutans. There are 150 adult females in the park. Estimate how many young will be born. To find out, multiply the fraction by the number of adult females.

(1) Multiply the numerator of the fraction by the whole number.

$$150 \text{ females} \times \frac{2 \text{ births}}{5 \text{ females}} = \frac{150 \times 2}{5} = \frac{300}{5}$$

(2) Divide by the denominator.

$$\frac{300}{5} = 300 \div 5 = 60$$

ANSWER 60 young

Answer the following questions.

1. In 2001, there were about 72 adult female right whales. Scientists observing the whales reported a 1/3 birth rate. About how many right whales were born in 2001?

2. Giant pandas are severely endangered. Currently about 140 giant pandas live in captivity, in zoos and parks. About 3/5 of these were born in captivity. How many is that?

3. The orangutan population of the world has decreased sharply. At one time there were over 100,000 ranging across Asia. Now there may be 21,000, of which, 2/3 live in Borneo. About how many orangutans live in Borneo?

CHALLENGE Suppose 1/1 is given as the desired birth rate to save an endangered population. If the population is currently at 4 births per 20 adult females, by how many times does the rate need to increase to reach the desired rate?

the BIG idea

Living things within an ecosystem interact with each other and the environment.

CONTENT REVIEW
CLASSZONE.COM

KEY CONCEPTS SUMMARY

2.1 **Groups of living things interact within ecosystems.**

- Members of the same species form a population within a habitat.

- Each species has a distinct role within a habitat. This is its niche.

Population of Crabs

Island Habitat for Crabs

VOCABULARY
species p. 45
population p. 46
habitat p. 46
niche p. 47
community p. 48

2.2 **Organisms can interact in different ways.**

Organisms within a community interact with each other in many ways. Some are predators, some are prey. Some compete with one another, some cooperate. Some species form symbiotic relationships with other species:

Mutualism
benefits both

Commensalism
benefits one, other unaffected

Parasitism
benefits one, harms other

VOCABULARY
predator p. 55
prey p. 55
competition p. 55
cooperation p. 57
symbiosis p. 58
mutualism p. 58
commensalism p. 59
parasitism p. 59

2.3 **Ecosystems are always changing.**

Primary Succession

In a barren area, a new community is established with pioneer species, like mosses, that do well with little or no soil. Mosses eventually give way to coniferous trees.

Secondary Succession

When a disturbance damages a community but soil remains, the community gets reestablished from seeds and roots left behind. Grasses grow, then small shrubs, and eventually trees.

VOCABULARY
limiting factor p. 64
carrying capacity p. 65
succession p. 66
pioneer species p. 66

Reviewing Vocabulary

Draw a Venn diagram for each pair of terms. Put shared characteristics in the overlap area, put differences to the outside. A sample diagram is provided.

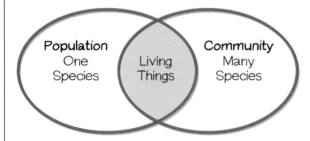

1. habitat, niche

2. mutualism, commensalism

3. mutualism, parasitism

4. competition, cooperation

5. primary succession, secondary succession

Reviewing Key Concepts

Multiple Choice *Choose the letter of the best answer.*

6. What is carrying capacity?
   a. the largest population an ecosystem can support
   b. the smallest population an ecosystem can support
   c. the number of species an ecosystem can support
   d. the number of habitats in an ecosystem

7. A new species of bird moves into a habitat. The birds feed on a particular caterpillar, so that the resulting population of butterflies is small. What can be said of the relationship between the birds and the butterflies?
   a. The birds and the butterflies have a commensal relationship.
   b. The birds and butterflies compete.
   c. The birds are a limiting factor for the butterflies.
   d. The birds and butterflies cooperate.

8. Certain types of worms live in the mud at the bottom of lakes. What does the mud represent for the worm?
   a. an ecosystem
   b. a niche
   c. a community
   d. a habitat

9. What is a pioneer species?
   a. a species that travels within an ecosystem
   b. a species that is among the first to move into an area after a natural disaster
   c. a species that depends upon animal life
   d. a species that cannot return after a natural disaster

10. Which is an example of competition within the same species?
    a. whales in a pod
    b. wildebeests in a herd
    c. creosote bushes in a desert
    d. birds that fly south

11. Which is an example of parasitism?
    a. dog and tick
    b. termite and protozoans
    c. shark and remora
    d. flower and hummingbird

12. Which is an example of secondary succession?
    a. succession after a forest fire
    b. succession after a large volcanic lava flow devastates an area
    c. succession after a glacier retreats, leaving bare rock
    d. succession after a hurricane washes away all the sand from a beach

Short Answer *Write a short answer to each question.*

13. Put the terms in order, starting with the term that includes the largest number of individuals and ending with the group containing the fewest individuals: community, population, ecosystem, biome.

14. List four ways in which members of the same species can cooperate with each other.

15. Describe three different types of symbiosis.

Thinking Critically

The data in the table below come from the records of a Canadian trading company that, in the late 1800s, bought lynx and hare pelts from hunters and trappers. The Canadian lynx and varying hare share the same habitat. The lynx relies on the hare as a food source. Use the table to answer the next three questions.

Year	Lynx	Hare
1	2	30
2	15	55
3	65	90
4	75	160
5	100	200
6	95	140
7	75	80
8	40	35
9	20	3
10	3	4
11	30	40
12	55	95

16. ANALYZE How would you describe the pattern that emerges between the two populations in years 1–7? How does the pattern change in years 8–10?

17. EVALUATE The data on the lynx and hare pelts have been used to suggest the sizes of the lynx and hare populations. Is this a reasonable approach to take? Why or why not?

18. ANALYZE Scientists have observed that hare populations will go through cycles of increasing and decreasing populations even when the lynx is not part of the habitat. How would you explain this observation?

19. APPLY A forest has pine trees, along with oak trees and birch trees. All the trees provide shelter and food for different animals in the habitat. Do these trees occupy the same niche? Explain.

20. INFER Explain why low-growing plants like mosses are eventually replaced by shrubs, and shrubs replaced by trees, in both primary and secondary successions.

21. PROVIDE EXAMPLES List three human activities that could lead to secondary succession.

22. ANALYZE Creosote bushes in the Mojave desert are spread out, so that each plant is about an equal distance from another. Write a short paragraph to describe the interaction of the creosote bushes, using the terms from the table.

competition	population pattern
limiting factor	community

23. APPLY How might building homes in a wooded area affect carrying capacity of different populations in the area?

the BIG idea

24. SUMMARIZE Look again at the photograph on pages 42–43. How would you change or add details to your answer to the question on the photograph?

25. APPLY Imagine that you are an ecologist from another galaxy who arrives on Earth. Describe a human community using the terms that an Earth ecologist would use to describe a natural community. Your description should include at least three examples of interactions between individuals (whether the same or different species). Identify the biotic or abiotic factors that serve as limiting factors to human population growth. Also state whether you think the human population is at or below its carrying capacity—and why.

UNIT PROJECTS

By now you should have completed the following items for your unit project.

- questions that you have asked about the topic
- schedule showing when you will complete each step of your project
- list of resources including Web sites, print resources, and materials

Understanding Symbiosis

Read the following description of the strangler fig and the relationship it has with other species in a rain forest. Then answer the questions that follow.

Strangler figs are part of many symbiotic relationships in a rain-forest ecosystem. In some cases, the symbiotic relationship benefits both the fig and an animal. Fig wasps lay their eggs in the fruit of the strangler fig and, in turn, pollinate it. Many birds feed on the fruit of the strangler fig and, in doing so, spread the seeds of the plant. The fig does not benefit from its interactions with all species. For example, certain butterflies feed on juice from the fruit without affecting the tree in any way.

The symbiotic relationship that gives the strangler fig its name is that between the strangler fig and its host tree. Birds drop seeds onto the top of a tree, and vines of the fig grow downward. Eventually, the vines of the strangler fig touch the ground and join with the roots of the host tree. The host tree is harmed because the leaves of the strangler fig block sunlight and its vines take root, using up nutrients the host tree needs.

1. Which feeding relationship is a form of mutualism in which both species benefit?
   a. the strangler fig and its host tree
   b. the strangler fig and the butterflies
   c. the strangler fig and the birds
   d. the strangler fig and the fig wasp

2. Which symbiotic relationship is a form of parasitism in which one species benefits and the other is harmed?
   a. the strangler fig and its host tree
   b. the strangler fig and the butterflies
   c. the strangler fig and the birds
   d. the strangler fig and the fig wasp

3. Which symbiotic relationship is a commensal relationship in which one species benefits without affecting the other?
   a. the strangler fig and its host tree
   b. the strangler fig and the butterflies
   c. the strangler fig and the birds
   d. the strangler fig and the fig wasp

4. Which word best describes the interaction between the strangler fig and its host?
   a. coexistence
   b. cooperation
   c. competition
   d. community

Extended Response

5. Strangler figs attach to trees that are sometimes cut for lumber. Write a paragraph that describes how removal of the host trees would affect these populations.
   • butterflies
   • birds
   • wasps
   • strangler figs

6. Write a paragraph describing some of the different roles played by a strangler fig in the rain forest. Use the vocabulary terms listed below in your answer.

habitat	niche	populations
community	ecosystem	

TIMELINES in Science

WILDERNESS CONSERVATION

The idea of wilderness conservation would have seemed strange to anyone living before the 1800s. The wilderness was vast and much of the wildlife in it dangerous to humans.

In the late 1800s, as smoke from railroads and factories rose in American skies, scientists, artists, even presidents began the work of setting aside land as parks and reservations to protect natural landscapes. Forestry, unpracticed in the U.S. before the 1890s, became a priority of the federal government as the new century dawned. Industries learned to harvest and nurture forests rather than clearing them. Next came the protection of animal species along with a call to control the pollution and depletion caused by human activity.

1872

National Parks Protect Resources

On March 1, 1872, President Ulysses S. Grant signs a law declaring Yellowstone's 2 million acres in northwest Wyoming as the country's first national park. Yellowstone serves as a model, and by 1887, about 45 million acres of forest have been set aside.

EVENTS

1870

APPLICATIONS and TECHNOLOGY

TECHNOLOGY

Seeing the Wilderness

Developments in photography in 1839, and its spread during the Civil War, led to adventurous mobile photographers in the late 1800s. In the early 1860s Mathew Brady and other photographers took mobile studios to the battlefields to bring war news to the public. By the late 1860s and early 1870s the wagonload shrank to a pack load. In 1871, William Henry Jackson balanced his tripod in Yellowstone, as the official photographer of the region's first U.S. Geological Survey.

1898

U.S. Division of Forestry Formed

Gifford Pinchot becomes the first chief of the Division of Forestry. Pinchot warns lumberers to abandon clear-cutting, urging them to practice forestry, a more scientific approach. Pinchot instructs lumberers "to have trees harvested when they are ripe."

1892

Sierra Club Founded

The Sierra Club is formed to help people explore and enjoy the mountains of the Pacific region. The Club's goal, with John Muir the unanimous choice for President, is to help people and government preserve the forests of the Sierra Nevada.

1916

National Park Service (NPS) Founded

The system of protected forests grows so big that a federal agency is formed to oversee it. Stephen Mather serves as its first director. Today the NPS employs 20,000 staff; has 90,000 volunteers; and oversees 83.6 million acres.

| 1880 | 1890 | 1900 | 1910 |

APPLICATION

Protecting Animal Species

Fashions of the 1890s used feathers, furs, even whole birds. Out of concern for the extinction of many birds, including the Carolina parakeet and the heath hen, a movement to stop wearing rare feathers began at small tea parties. The U.S. Congress enacted the Lacey Act in 1900 to restore endangered species of game and wild birds. The landmark act became the first in a century of laws protecting animals. The Migratory Bird Treaty of 1918, the Bald Eagle Act of 1940, and the Endangered Species Act of 1973 set animal conservation as a national priority. The Endangered Species Act met its strongest test in protecting the northern spotted owl, whose entire range—in California, Oregon, Washington, and Canada—is protected.

1951
Nature Conservancy Established
The Nature Conservancy is formed to preserve plants, animals, and natural communities that represent Earth's biological diversity.

1963
Glen Canyon Destroyed
Completion of the Glen Canyon dam causes flooding in Glen Canyon, an immense area north of the Grand Canyon. Many groups fight to close the dam, but it is too late. The canyon is destroyed as Lake Powell forms.

1962
Silent Spring *Breaks Silence*
Biologist and science writer Rachel Carson publishes *Silent Spring.* Chemical pesticides have been widely used and publicized, but Carson uses scientific evidence to show that many of these chemicals harm people and the environment.

1968
Grand Canyon Dam Plans Squashed
Plans to dam the Grand Canyon are withdrawn as a result of public outcry. Recalling what happened to Glen Canyon, organizers ran national newspaper ads in 1966 making the public aware of plans to dam the Canyon.

1950   **1960**   **1970**

TECHNOLOGY

Maps to Save the Wilderness
Land and wildlife conservation has benefited from computer-based mapping technology called global information systems (GIS). GIS compiles satellite photographs, temperature readings, and other information into a central set of data. Scientists enter distributions of animals and overlay these data on existing maps. The resulting GIS maps show the gap in an animal's range and the quality of its habitat. Government efforts to restore the habitat of the endangered San Joaquin Kit Fox relied on GIS maps.

1980 to present
Reservation vs. Resource

In 1980, Congress expands the Arctic National Wildlife Refuge (ANWR) to more than twice its 1960 size. In 2001, President George W. Bush proposes limited oil drilling within the range. Today, debate continues over how to manage its resources and wildlife.

RESOURCE CENTER
CLASSZONE.COM

Read more about current conservation efforts.

1990   2000

INTO THE FUTURE

Society has long put a price on natural resources—minerals, water, timber, and so on. But how much is an ecosystem worth? Communities have begun to look at the dollar values of "ecosystem services," the ongoing activities in nature that keep our environment healthy. Data is needed on ecosystem processes. Such data can be compared to the services of human-made treatment plants and agriculture.

Other questions arise with protecting species. Many species, such as wild turkeys and bald eagles, once endangered have come back in great numbers. When a protected species thrives it may endanger another species or bump up against the human landscape and human activity. How can managers of resources set priorities?

APPLICATION
Selling a Service

In New York City in 1996, the water department spent $1.5 billion to protect natural watersheds rather than build a $6 billion water treatment plant. In 2001, a group of scientists met to promote the value that ecosystems bring to society—benefits that include pest control, air purification, and water treatment. For example, dragonflies can eat 300 mosquitoes in a single day. Toads and bats can eat a thousand or more mosquitoes in a single day or night.

ACTIVITIES

Ecosystem Services Proposal

What services to the human population are provided by your local ecosystem? Choose one service and describe how natural processes and interactions within the ecosystem provide the benefits you've identified. What processes are involved?

Write a proposal for protecting the ecosystem. Include a comparison of the estimated cost of protecting the ecosystem and the cost of human services that provide a similar benefit.

Writing Project: The Story Behind the News

Research one of the events described on the timeline. Then write the story behind that event.

Human Impact on Ecosystems

the **BIG** idea

Humans and human population growth affect the environment.

How have humans affected this landscape?

Key Concepts

SECTION

(3.1) Human population growth presents challenges.
Learn how the increasing human population must share land and resources and dispose of its wastes.

SECTION

(3.2) Human activities affect the environment.
Learn how humans may affect natural resources, air and water quality, and biodiversity.

SECTION

(3.3) People are working to protect ecosystems.
Learn about federal, local, and scientific efforts to improve resource use and protect ecosystems.

 Internet Preview

 CLASSZONE.COM

Chapter 3 online resources: Content Review, Visualization, four Resource Centers, Math Tutorial, Test Practice

How Many Is Six Billion?

Use a piece of paper, scissors, and some tape to make a box that measures 1 cm by 1 cm by 1 cm. Fill the box with rice. Use the number of grains of rice in 1 cm^3 to calculate the volume of 6,000,000,000 grains of rice.

Observe and Think How many grains of rice are in a cubic centimeter? Do 6 billion grains take up more or less space than you expected?

How Easily Does Polluted Water Move Through Plants?

Place a few drops of food coloring in a half cup of water. Take a leafy stalk of celery and make a fresh cut across the bottom. Place the celery in the water overnight.

Observe and Think What do you observe about the celery and its leaves? What do your observations suggest about plants growing near polluted water?

Internet Activity: The Environment

Go to **ClassZone.com** to explore the effects of human activities on the environment.

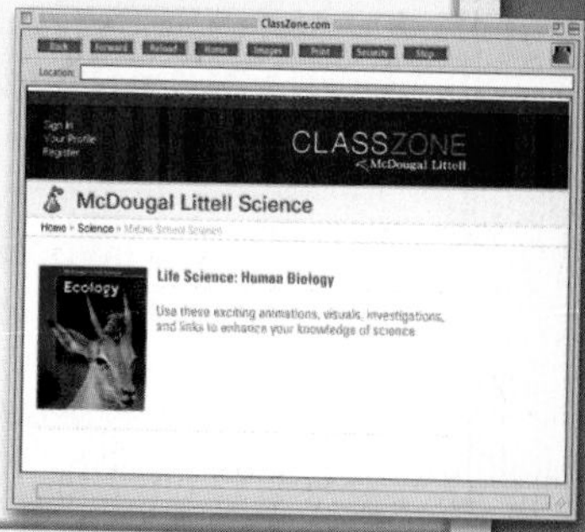

Observe and Think How are people working to protect the environment?

NSTA
scilinks.org
SCiLINKS

Population Growth Code: MDL003

Getting Ready to Learn

◀ CONCEPT REVIEW

- Both living and nonliving factors affect ecosystems.
- Populations can grow or decline over time.
- Matter and energy move through the environment.

◀ VOCABULARY REVIEW

species p. 45

habitat p. 46

See Glossary for definitions.

diversity, urban

CONTENT REVIEW
CLASSZONE.COM
Review concepts and vocabulary.

▶ TAKING NOTES

SUPPORTING MAIN IDEAS

Make a chart to show main ideas and the information that supports them. Copy each blue heading; then add supporting information, such as reasons, explanations, and examples.

VOCABULARY STRATEGY

Think about a vocabulary term as a **magnet word** diagram. Write the other terms or ideas related to that term around it.

See the Note-Taking Handbook on pages R45–R51.

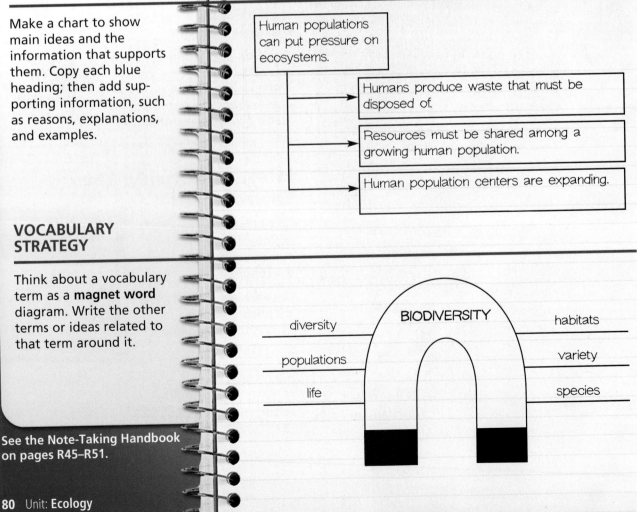

SCIENCE NOTEBOOK

Human populations can put pressure on ecosystems.

→ Humans produce waste that must be disposed of.

→ Resources must be shared among a growing human population.

→ Human population centers are expanding.

diversity   BIODIVERSITY   habitats

populations   variety

life   species

Human population growth presents challenges.

BEFORE, you learned

- Populations have boundaries and are affected by limiting factors
- Living things form communities

NOW, you will learn

- How a growing human population puts pressure on ecosystems
- How sharing resources can be difficult

VOCABULARY

natural resource p. 84
population density p. 86

EXPLORE Sharing Resources

How can you model resource distribution?

PROCEDURE

MATERIALS
bag containing an assortment of objects

1. You will work in a group of several classmates. One member of your group gets a bag of objects from your teacher.

2. Each object in the bag represents a necessary resource. Divide the objects so that each member of the group gets the resources he or she needs.

3. After 10 minutes, you may trade resources with other groups.

WHAT DO YOU THINK?

- Did you get a fair share of your group's objects?
- How does the number of people in each group affect the outcome?
- Was the job made easier when trading occurred across groups?

 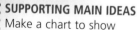

SUPPORTING MAIN IDEAS
Make a chart to show information that supports the first main idea presented: *The human population is increasing.*

The human population is increasing.

According to the United Nations, on October 12, 1999, Earth's human population reached 6 billion. Until 300 years ago, it had never grown beyond a few hundred million people. Only 200 years ago, the population reached 1 billion. So the increase to 6 billion people has occurred in a very short time. About one-third of all humans alive today are 14 years old or younger. Partly for this reason, experts predict Earth's population will keep growing—to 9 billion or more by the year 2050.

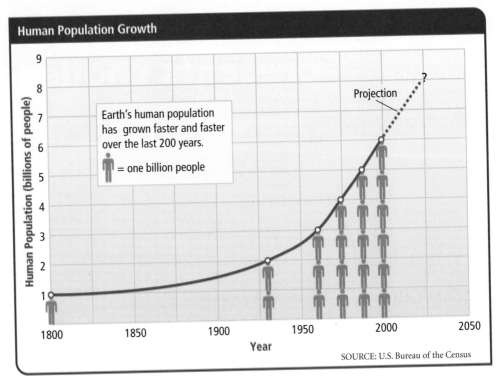

Human Population Growth

Earth's human population has grown faster and faster over the last 200 years.

 = one billion people

Projection

Human Population (billions of people)

Year

SOURCE: U.S. Bureau of the Census

PREDICT The graph shows actual population growth through 2000. Predict how the population will grow in the future.

The graph above shows how the human population has grown in the last 200 years. You can see from the way the graph gets noticeably steeper after 1950 how quickly the population has increased in just the last 50 years. It is not just the number of babies being born that contributes to Earth's large human population. People are living longer as a result of improving health care and nutrition.

The dotted line on the graph shows a projection, which helps us predict what the population would be if it continues to grow at the rate it is growing today. However, remember that an ecosystem has a carrying capacity for any given population. At some point, Earth will reach its carrying capacity for the human population. Today, many people think that our planet is close to—if not already at—its carrying capacity for humans.

CHECK YOUR READING How might Earth's carrying capacity affect human population growth?

Human populations can put pressure on ecosystems.

VISUALIZATION
CLASSZONE.COM

Examine how the human population has grown.

If your family has guests for the weekend, you may find that you run out of hot water for showers or do not have enough milk for everyone's breakfast. The resources that would ordinarily be enough for your family are no longer enough.

You read in Chapter 2 that resources such as food, water, and space can be limiting factors for biological populations. These same resources limit Earth's human population. As the human population grows, it uses more resources—just as your weekend visitors used more of your home's resources. The activities of the growing human population are putting pressure on Earth's ecosystems.

▼ REMINDER

A *limiting factor* is something that prevents a population from continuing to grow.

Pressures of Waste Disposal

As Earth's human population grows, so does the amount of waste produced by humans. Humans, like all living things, produce natural waste. Often, the water that carries this waste is treated to remove harmful chemicals before being cycled back to the environment. However, some of these materials still make it into lakes, rivers, and oceans, harming these ecosystems.

Much of the waste material produced by humans is the result of human activity. Some of this waste is garbage, or food waste. The rest of it is trash, or nonfood waste. In the United States, huge amounts of trash are thrown out each year. Most garbage and trash ends up in landfills.

Landfills take up a lot of space. The Fresh Kills Landfill in Staten Island, New York, is 60 meters (197 ft) high and covers an area as big as 2200 football fields. Decomposing trash and garbage can release dangerous gases into the air as well as harmful chemicals into the ground. Liners, which are layers of plastic or packed clay, are used to keep chemicals from leaking into surrounding land and water.

Waste is deposited in one area at a time.

Each layer is covered with soil and clay.

Liners at the base of the landfill keep harmful materials from leaking.

clay

groundwater

Another way to get rid of trash and garbage is to incinerate it—burn it. The problem with incineration is that it releases harmful gases and chemicals into the air. To prevent the release of these harmful substances, incinerator smokestacks have filters. To prevent further environmental contamination, used filters must be disposed of safely.

Pressures on Resources

You have seen that a growing human population puts pressure on ecosystems by the amount of waste it leaves behind. Human populations also put pressure on ecosystems by what they take away. Humans depend on the environment for resources. A **natural resource** is any type of material or energy that humans use to meet their needs. Natural resources that humans take from their environment include water, food, wood, stone, metal, and minerals.

Clean fresh water is an important resource. Only 3 percent of Earth's water supply is fresh water—and two-thirds of that small amount is locked up in polar ice caps, glaciers, and permanent snow. As the human population grows, sharing this important resource will become more difficult.

INVESTIGATE Resources

How does your community meet its needs?

PROCEDURE

1. Obtain a recent map of your county, city, or town.

2. Using the map, try to identify where your community gets its electricity and water and how it disposes of trash and garbage.

3. Identify locations where food is grown.

WHAT DO YOU THINK?

- How much does your community rely on other communities for resources?
- What resources does your community share with other communities?
- Where does your community dispose of its own waste materials?

CHALLENGE Draw a grid on a piece of tracing paper and place it on top of the map. Use your grid to estimate what percentage of land in your city or town is used for housing and what percentage is used for governmental, agricultural, and commercial purposes.

SKILL FOCUS
Interpreting

MATERIALS
- map of your county, city, or town
For Challenge:
- tracing paper
- pencil
- ruler

TIME
30 minutes

Case Study: The Colorado River

The dark green area shows the watershed of the Colorado River.

WYOMING

NEVADA

UTAH

Colorado R.

CALIFORNIA

COLORADO

PACIFIC OCEAN

Colorado R.

NEW MEXICO

ARIZONA

0   100   200 miles
0   100   200 kilometers

I Major dam
   Watershed

MEXICO

A lot of water flows in the upper parts of the Colorado River.

Little water flows through this wide riverbed in Mexico.

A case study that involves the Colorado River shows how a growing human population puts pressures on natural resources. This example also shows that sharing resources isn't easy. The watershed of this major Western river extends into seven U.S. states and parts of Mexico. The watershed includes all the smaller rivers and streams that flow into the Colorado River. In a region where little rain falls each year, these streams and rivers are an important source of water for drinking and agriculture.

As the West was settled, people in the downstream states of California, Arizona, and Nevada worried that the people in the upstream states of Colorado, Utah, Wyoming, and New Mexico would drain too much water from the river. In 1922 the seven states signed an agreement that divided the water between the two groups.

Problems with this agreement soon became apparent. First, the needs of Native American and Mexican populations were not considered. Second, the dams and channels built to prevent floods and transport water harmed river ecosystems. And third, the seven states planned to use more water than the river usually holds. As a result, the river often runs nearly dry at its mouth, in Mexico.

READING TIP

As you read about the Colorado River, refer to the map above to see where the river flows and the states that use the Colorado River's water.

 CHECK YOUR READING

List three problems that developed after people made a plan to share Colorado River water.

Pressures of Urban Growth

 RESOURCE CENTER
CLASSZONE.COM

Learn more about urban expansion.

Until recently, the majority of Earth's population was spread out, so the population density was low. **Population density** is the measure of the number of people in a given area. Generally, the lower the population density, the less pressure there is on the environment.

Today, about half of the world's population lives in urban, or city, areas. People are attracted to these areas to live and to work. Over time, suburban areas around a city develop as more and more people look for a place to live. In cities, buildings are spaced close together, so the population density is high. A large number of people in a small area changes the landscape. The local environment can no longer support the number of people living there, and so resources must come from outside.

CHECK YOUR READING How does population density in a city differ from the population density of a suburb?

In recent years, some people have raised concern over the dramatic growth in and around urban areas. Los Angeles; Houston; Atlanta; and Washington, D.C. are all cities that have rapidly expanded. Another urban area that has experienced dramatic growth is Las Vegas, Nevada. The images below show the effects of increasing

Las Vegas, 1972

The darker colors distinguish the developed land of Las Vegas from the surrounding desert.

Las Vegas, 1997

city center

Over 25 years, the city expanded in all directions. The population went from 273,000 to 1,124,000.

population density around the city between 1972 and 1997. Located in the middle of the desert, Las Vegas depends upon the Colorado River for water and electrical energy. As the population grows, so does the need for natural resources.

Pressures of Expanding Land Use

An increasing demand for resources in a particular area is one consequence of urban growth. But as communities around cities expand onto surrounding land, the environment is affected. Natural habitats, such as forests, are destroyed. Because forests cycle carbon through the environment, cutting down trees affects the carbon cycle. Soil that was held in place by tree roots may wash into lakes and rivers.

Another consequence of widespread development is the loss of productive farmland. Development replaces more than 2.5 million acres of farmland each year in the United States. This means less land is available locally to produce food for the growing population. The result is that food is often transported great distances.

Unlike compact city development, widespread suburban development also increases the need for residents to have cars. This is because most people in suburban areas live farther from where they work, shop, or go to school. A greater number of cars decreases the air quality in communities and requires additional road construction, which can interrupt natural habitats and endanger wildlife.

INFER What do you think this ecosystem looked like a hundred years ago? two hundred years ago?

⬤ **CHECK YOUR READING** Describe some ways that development harms natural ecosystems.

3.1 Review

KEY CONCEPTS

1. Identify four pressures placed on ecosystems by an increasing human population.

2. Give an example that shows how resources can be difficult to share.

CRITICAL THINKING

3. **Apply** Describe an example of sharing resources that occurs in your home.

4. **Infer** How would a city's population density change if the city increased in area and the number of people in it remained the same?

⬤ CHALLENGE

5. **Evaluate** Imagine that you lived along the Colorado River. What information would you need if you wanted to evaluate a water-sharing agreement?

Ecology in Urban Planning

Urban planners design and locate buildings, transportation systems, and green spaces in cities. One important thing they consider is how their proposal for development will affect the ecosystem. With the help of ecology, urban planners can balance the needs of humans and the environment.

1 GATHERING DATA Urban planners use maps to gather information about the layout of a city, where populations of plants and animals exist, and where water and land resources are located.

2 ANALYZING DATA Scientists help urban planners determine how the location and density of buildings, roads, or parks can affect natural habitats.

3 APPLYING DATA By understanding the ecosystem, urban planners can develop areas to support different needs.

This habitat is left untouched because it supports rare migrating birds. Development would disturb the ecosystem and put the birds at risk.

This area has a stable population of native species. Park benches and trails encourage human recreation in well defined areas.

EXPLORE

1. **APPLY** Both ecologists and urban planners have to understand the ways that biotic and abiotic factors are interconnected. List some biotic and abiotic factors in a human community.

2. **CHALLENGE** Use the Internet to find out more about the planning board or planning office in your community. Is your community growing? In what ways? What are some decisions that planners are helping to make?

KEY CONCEPT
Human activities affect the environment.

BEFORE, you learned

- Human populations are increasing
- Human population growth causes problems

NOW, you will learn

- How natural resources are classified
- How pollution affects the environment
- How a loss of diversity affects the environment

VOCABULARY

pollution p. 91
biodiversity p. 91

THINK ABOUT

How do you use water?

Think of the number of times you use water every day. Like all living things, you need water. In fact, more than half of the material that makes up your body is water.

No matter where you live, most of the time you can turn on a faucet and clean water flows out the spout. You use water when you take a shower, fix a snack, or wash a dish. If you've ever lost water service to your home, you've probably been reminded how much you depend upon it. No doubt about it, our need for water is serious.

SUPPORTING MAIN IDEAS
Make a chart to show information that supports the main idea: *Humans use many resources.*

Humans use many resources.

Throughout history, people around the world have relied on natural resources for survival. Ancient civilizations used stone to create tools and weapons. And wood was an important fuel for cooking and keeping warm. Today, humans continue to rely on the environment and have discovered additional resources to meet their needs. In Section 3.1 you read about sharing natural resources. Scientists classify these resources into two categories:

- renewable resources
- nonrenewable resources

Renewable Resources

RESOURCE CENTER
CLASSZONE.COM

Find out more about natural resources.

Two hundred years ago, most small towns in the Northeastern part of the United States included farm fields, pasture, and woods. The wooded areas that weren't farmed were used as wood lots. The wood from these lots supplied firewood for towns and was often exported for income.

Trees are an example of a renewable resource—a resource that can be used over and over again. Energy from sunlight is another important renewable resource. Because the Sun is expected to supply energy for another five billion years, energy from sunlight is considered essentially unlimited. As you read earlier in your study of the water cycle, water can be classified as a renewable resource. Renewable resources can be replaced naturally or by humans in a short amount of time, but they may run out if they are overused or managed poorly.

 CHECK YOUR READING Give three examples of renewable resources. Explain why each one is considered renewable.

Nonrenewable Resources

Nonrenewable resources are resources that cannot be replaced. In some cases, they may be replenished by natural processes, but not quickly enough for human purposes. Nonrenewable resources are often underground, making them more difficult to reach. But technology has enabled humans to locate and remove nonrenewable resources from places that used to be impossible to reach.

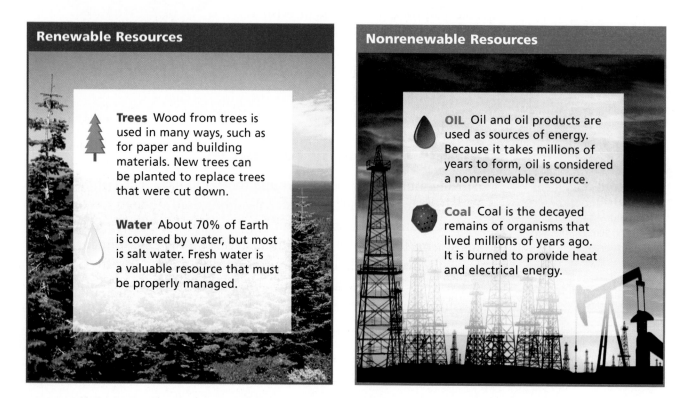

Renewable Resources

Trees Wood from trees is used in many ways, such as for paper and building materials. New trees can be planted to replace trees that were cut down.

Water About 70% of Earth is covered by water, but most is salt water. Fresh water is a valuable resource that must be properly managed.

Nonrenewable Resources

OIL Oil and oil products are used as sources of energy. Because it takes millions of years to form, oil is considered a nonrenewable resource.

Coal Coal is the decayed remains of organisms that lived millions of years ago. It is burned to provide heat and electrical energy.

Coal, petroleum, and natural gas are nonrenewable resources that are removed from underground by mining or drilling. Also called fossil fuels, they are the main energy source for heating, industry, and transportation and are used to make many products. Many minerals, like copper and gold, are also considered nonrenewable resources.

Pollution endangers biodiversity.

As you walk along a city street, you may smell exhaust or see litter. These are examples of pollution. **Pollution** is the addition of harmful substances to the environment. Many of the ways humans use natural resources cause pollution to be released into the soil, air, and water. Pollutants include chemicals, bacteria, and dirt. Even materials that are ordinarily not harmful can cause pollution when they build up in one location.

As pollution becomes common in an ecosystem, living things may be threatened. Plant and animal populations may decrease and biodiversity may decline. **Biodiversity** is the number and variety of life forms within an ecosystem. Healthy ecosystems support a variety of species. An ecosystem with a variety of organisms can recover more easily from disturbances than an ecosystem that has fewer species.

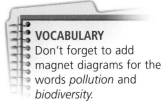

VOCABULARY
Don't forget to add magnet diagrams for the words *pollution* and *biodiversity*.

INVESTIGATE Particles in the Air

Where do you find air pollution?

PROCEDURE

1. Use a hole punch to make holes at the ends of two index cards. Cut two pieces of string 30 cm long and tie one string to each card.

2. Choose a different location for each card. Mark the card with its location and the date.

3. Spread a thin film of petroleum jelly on a 3 cm^2 area on each card and hang each card at the location you've chosen.

4. Collect the cards in one week and examine them with the hand lens.

WHAT DO YOU THINK?

- Identify the types of particles collected at each location.
- Do you think of all of the particles collected as pollution?
- Which location had the most pollution?

CHALLENGE Hypothesize why certain locations have more particles in the air than others.

SKILL FOCUS
Observing

MATERIALS
- 2 index cards
- marker
- hole punch
- string
- scissors
- petroleum jelly
- hand lens

TIME
30 minutes

Air Quality

Air quality affects entire ecosystems. For example, in 1980, Mount St. Helens erupted on the West Coast of the United States. Hot ash was blown 15 miles up into the air. Three days later some of that ash reached the East Coast. Although natural events occasionally release air pollutants, human activities pollute every day.

READING TiP

Pollute and *pollutant* are in the same word family as pollution.

Today in the United States, motor vehicles, factories, and power plants are the main sources of air pollution. The fossil fuels they burn release sulfur dioxide, nitrogen dioxide, and carbon monoxide into the air. These pollutants affect humans and animals and are the main cause of acid rain, a serious problem affecting ecosystems.

 CHECK YOUR READING What air pollutants contribute to acid rain problems in the United States?

Acid rain occurs when air pollutants such as sulfur dioxide and nitrogen dioxide mix with water in the atmosphere to form acid droplets of rain, ice, snow, or mist. Just as the wind carried ash from Mount St. Helens, wind can carry these droplets for very long distances before they fall as rain.

Acid rain has been very harmful in areas without rich soil to help correct the rain's acidity. In New York's Adirondack Mountains, acid rain has killed all the fish in some lakes. The photograph below shows the impact of acid rain on trees in the Adirondacks. Where acid rain falls, it damages leaves and soil. This damage destroys both habitats and food sources for many animals, eventually reducing biodiversity.

Acid-Rain Damage

A close look at the branch reveals that some of the needles are turning brown.

Air Quality Spruce trees in the Adirondacks show damage caused when pollutants in the air mix with rain.

Water Quality

Water quality is another factor that affects biodiversity in ecosystems. Forty years ago, newspaper headlines announced that Lake Erie was "dead" because of pollution. Almost every living thing in the lake had died. Lake Erie suffered for years from pollution by neighborhoods, industries, and farms along its banks. Rivers that emptied into the lake also carried pollution with them.

The pollution found in Lake Erie is common in communities across the United States. Chemicals or waste that drain off of farm fields, animal feedlots, and landfills all cause water pollution. So do oil spills, soil erosion, and the discharging of wastewater from towns and industries.

CHECK YOUR READING Name four different sources of water pollution.

Like air pollution, water pollution affects entire ecosystems. One river that suffers from heavy pollution is the Duwamish River in Washington. Over 600 million gallons of untreated waste and storm water drain off the land into the river. As a result, large amounts of bacteria and harmful chemicals contaminate the water, killing fish and putting humans at risk.

When fish and amphibians in aquatic ecosystems are exposed to pollution, the entire food web is affected. If fish become scarce, some birds may no longer find enough food. The bird population may decrease as birds die or move to a new habitat. The result is that biodiversity in the ecosystem decreases.

Water Quality A scientist tests the water of the Duwamish River after chemicals were released into the river.

Chemical Pollution

Pollution that flows into aquatic ecosystems can harm—even kill—organisms like these fish.

Pollution Across Systems

As you have learned, pollution can be spread among ecosystems by abiotic factors. For example, wind carried ash from Mount St. Helens to different ecosystems. Wind also carries acid rain to forest ecosystems. Pollution can also move between air and water. For example, some chemical pollutants can run off land and into a body of water. These pollutants, like the water itself, can evaporate from the water's surface and cycle into the air, moving into the atmosphere.

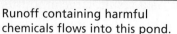

water carries pollutants

① Runoff containing harmful chemicals flows into this pond.

air carries pollutants

② The chemicals evaporate into the air from the surface of the water.

Habitat loss endangers biodiversity.

Scientists know that an ecosystem with many different species of plants and animals can withstand the effects of flooding, drought, and disease more effectively than an ecosystem with fewer species. But for biodiversity to be maintained, a habitat must be able to support a large number of different species. If living space is limited or a food source is removed, then the number of species in a biological community will be reduced.

Removing Habitat

One way human activities affect habitats is by reducing the amounts of natural resources available to living things. When this occurs, populations that rely on those resources are less likely to survive. For example, if you trim all the dead branches off the trees in your yard and remove them, insects that live in rotting wood will not settle in your yard. As a result, woodpeckers that may have nested in the area will lose their source of food. By removing this food source, you might affect the biodiversity in your backyard.

Now consider altering an ecosystem much larger than your backyard. Instead of removing a single resource, imagine removing a large area of land that is a habitat to many different species. Disturbing habitats removes not only food but space, shelter, and protection for living things.

Removing Habitat

A clear-cut forest provides a dramatic example of habitat loss.

Forest Habitat The forest provides food and shelter for many organisms.

Deforestation Removing all the trees from an area removes habitat that other species depend on.

Because of land development, forests that once stretched for hundreds of miles have been fragmented, or broken apart into small patches. Organisms that depend on trees cannot live in woods that have large areas that have been clear-cut. Their habitat is removed or reduced so there is a greater risk of attack by predators. Skunks, raccoons, and crows, which eat the eggs of forest songbirds, will not travel deep into large forests. However, they can reach nests more easily when forests are broken into small areas.

CHECK YOUR READING Why is biodiversity important and how can human activities affect it?

Changing Habitat

Another kind of habitat loss occurs when humans move species into new habitats, either on purpose or by accident. Some species, when released in a new place, successfully compete against the native species, crowding them out. Over time, these species, called invasive species, may replace the native species.

One example of an invasive plant is purple loosestrife. In the 1800s loosestrife from Europe was brought to the United States to use as a garden plant and medicinal herb. One loosestrife plant can make about 2 million seeds a year. These seeds are carried long distances by wind, water, animals, and humans. Loosestrife sprouts in wetlands, where it can fill in open-water habitat or replace native plants such as goldenrod. Most ducks and fish do not feed on purple loosestrife.

Changing Habitat

Habitat loss occurs when purple loosestrife fills in open water or crowds out goldenrod.

Invasive Species Purple loosestrife fills in wetlands and crowds out native species, disturbing organisms that rely on native species for food or living space.

Native Species Goldenrod is a native species that is a food source for many wetland populations.

When the native plants that wetland animals depend on are crowded out by loosestrife, the animals disappear, too.

Scientists estimate that Earth supports more than 10 million different species. They also estimate that thousands of species are threatened, and over a hundred species of plants and animals become extinct every year. By protecting biodiversity we can help ecosystems thrive and even recover more quickly after a natural disturbance such as a hurricane. And biodiversity directly benefits humans. For example, many medications are based on natural compounds from plants that only grow in certain types of ecosystems.

3.2 Review

KEY CONCEPTS

1. List some renewable and nonrenewable resources that you need to survive.

2. Describe two ways in which pollution can move through ecosystems.

3. Explain what scientists mean by *biodiversity*.

CRITICAL THINKING

4. **Explain** Under some circumstances, valuable natural resources can be considered pollutants. Explain this statement, giving two examples.

5. **Compare** Identify two natural habitats in your area, one with high biodiversity and one with low biodiversity. Describe the biodiversity of each.

○ CHALLENGE

6. **Hypothesize** When lakes are polluted by acid rain, the water appears to become clearer, not cloudier. Why do you think this is the case?

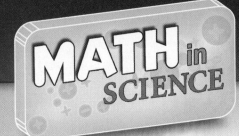

How Much Water?

When you take a 10-minute shower, you are using about 190 liters
of water. How much is that? Liters are a metric unit of capacity—
the amount of liquid that can fit into a container of a certain size.
The liter is based on a metric unit of volume. One liter is equal to
1000 cubic centimeters.

Example

A rectangular tank holds the amount of water used for a
10-minute shower. The dimensions of the tank are
250 cm × 40 cm × 19 cm. What is the volume of the tank?

Volume = **length** × **width** × **height**

$V = l \times w \times h$

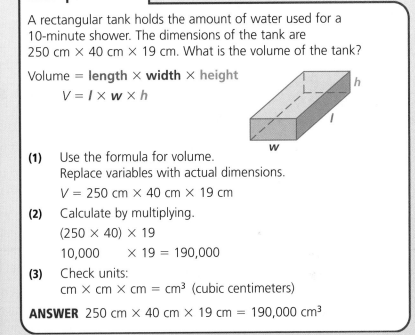

(1)   Use the formula for volume.
Replace variables with actual dimensions.

$V = 250 \text{ cm} \times 40 \text{ cm} \times 19 \text{ cm}$

(2)   Calculate by multiplying.

(250 × 40) × 19

10,000   × 19 = 190,000

(3)   Check units:
cm × cm × cm = cm³ (cubic centimeters)

ANSWER 250 cm × 40 cm × 19 cm = 190,000 cm³

Find the following volumes or dimensions.

1. Brushing your teeth with the water running uses the water in a
tank 14 cm by 45 cm by 12 cm. Sketch an aquarium that holds
exactly this amount. Label the dimensions. What is the volume?

2. If you turn off the water while you brush, you use only about
half as much water. Sketch a rectangular tank that holds this
volume. Label the dimensions. What is the volume?

3. A typical toilet flush uses the water in a 50 cm by 20 cm by
20 cm space. Find the volume in cubic centimeters. Sketch a
model of this volume.

CHALLENGE An Olympic swimming pool is 50 m by 25 m by
3 m. What is its volume? There are approximately 5678 cubic
meters of water in the water tower shown. How many
Olympic pools of water would it take to fill the tower?

3.3 People are working to protect ecosystems.

◀ BEFORE, you learned	▶ NOW, you will learn
• Human activities produce pollutants • Human activity is depleting some natural resources	• About some of the laws that have been passed to help protect the environment • About efforts that are being made to conserve natural resources

VOCABULARY

conservation p. 99
sustainable p. 102

EXPLORE Environmental Impacts

What happens when soil is compressed?

PROCEDURE

1. Fill two pots with 1 cup each of potting soil.

2. Compress the soil in the second pot by pushing down hard upon it with your hand.

3. Pour 1 cup of water into the first pot. Start the stopwatch as soon as you start pouring. Stop the watch as soon as all the water has been absorbed. Record the time.

4. Pour 1 cup of water into the second pot and again record how long it takes for the water to be absorbed. Wash your hands.

MATERIALS
• 2 plant pots with trays
• measuring cups
• potting soil
• water
• stopwatch

WHAT DO YOU THINK?
• What effect does compressing the soil have upon how quickly the water is absorbed?
• What might happen to water that is not absorbed quickly by soil?

Environmental awareness is growing.

SUPPORTING MAIN IDEAS
Make a chart to list some of the activities that show that environmental awareness is growing.

As people moved westward across grassy plains and steep mountain ranges of the United States, many believed our nation's resources were endless. Midwestern prairies were converted to farmland. Forests were clear-cut for lumber. Land was mined for coal.

By the 1800s, foresters and naturalists began to take interest in preserving the wild areas they saw rapidly disappearing. In 1872 our nation's outlook started to change when Yellowstone, the world's first national park, was established. It wasn't long before conservation of wild places became a goal. **Conservation** is the process of saving or protecting a natural resource.

RESOURCE CENTER
CLASSZONE.COM
Discover how people help ecosystems recover.

The movement to protect our environment grew rapidly in the 1960s. *Silent Spring,* a book that raised public awareness of the effect of harmful chemicals in the environment, sparked debate about serious pollution problems. As local efforts for environmental protection grew, the United States government responded. Throughout the 1970s important laws were passed to preserve and protect the environment. Today small groups of citizens, along with local and national government efforts, protect America's natural resources.

 List three events in the history of the environmental movement in the United States.

Volunteers work to clean up a stream.

Local Efforts

Maybe you have heard the expression "Think globally, act locally." It urges people to consider the health of the entire planet and to take action in their own communities. Long before federal and state agencies began enforcing environmental laws, individuals were coming together to protect habitats and the organisms that depend on them. These efforts are often referred to as grassroots efforts. They occur on a local level and are primarily run by volunteers.

Often the efforts of a few citizens gather the support and interest of so many people that they form a larger organization. These groups work to bring about change by communicating with politicians, publishing articles, or talking to the news media. Some groups purchase land and set it aside for preservation.

Federal Efforts

You have probably heard of the Endangered Species Act or the Clean Air Act. You might wonder, though, exactly what these laws do. The United States government works with scientists to write laws that ensure that companies and individuals work together to conserve natural resources and maintain healthy ecosystems.

In the late 1960s the National Environmental Policy Act, known as NEPA, made the protection of natural ecosystems a national goal. Several important laws followed. For example, the Clean Air Act and Clean Water Act improved the control of different kinds and amounts of pollutants that can be put into the air and water. The Environmental Protection Agency (EPA) enforces all federal environmental laws.

 CHECK YOUR READING Identify two federal environmental laws.

Over the past decades, chemical waste from factories has piled up in landfills and polluted water sources. These wastes can threaten ecosystems and human health. In 1980, citizen awareness of the dangers led to the Superfund Program. The goal of the program is to identify dangerous areas and to clean up the worst sites.

Helping Endangered Species

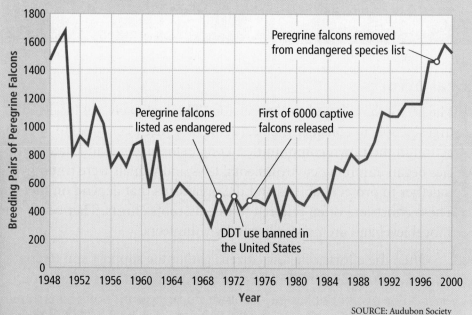

Government and private groups have helped peregrine falcon populations to recover.

Peregrine falcons removed from endangered species list

Peregrine falcons listed as endangered

First of 6000 captive falcons released

DDT use banned in the United States

Breeding Pairs of Peregrine Falcons

1800
1600
1400
1200
1000
800
600
400
200
0

1948 1952 1956 1960 1964 1968 1972 1976 1980 1984 1988 1992 1996 2000

Year

SOURCE: Audubon Society

Ecosystem Recovery

A growing awareness of the importance of healthy ecosystems is inspiring restoration projects.

Wetland

Restoration efforts in Galveston Bay, Texas, focus on bringing back the sea-grass meadows near the coast.

Volunteers help replant sea grass around Galveston Island State Park. Sea grass is a major habitat for birds, fish, and crabs and helps prevent erosion by holding bottom sediments in place.

Desert

Members of a restoration group work to restore desert plants and soil in Red Rock Canyon State Park, California.

1 A power auger is used to break up severely compacted soil and prepare it for planting.

2 Seedlings of native species, like the saltbush, are grown off site. Once they reach a more mature size, they are brought in to be planted.

3 Plastic cones are used to protect plants from being disturbed by severe weather or predators.

Federal agencies oversee the Superfund Program and other environmental laws. In addition to federal laws protecting the environment, there are state laws. Companies must follow all the laws that apply in each state where they do business. The same company may need to follow different laws in different states.

The United States is just one of many countries learning to deal with the effects of their human population on the environment. Dozens of countries have already met to discuss concerns about clear-cutting, water pollution, and endangered species. At this international level, the United Nations Environment Programme encourages sound environmental practices worldwide.

INFER At this Superfund site, the chemical cadmium pollutes the soil. Why does this worker need to wear a face mask?

Conserving resources protects ecosystems.

Around the world, individuals and companies are expressing more interest in **sustainable** practices—ways of living and doing business that use natural resources without using them up. Sustainable development allows people to enjoy a high quality of life while limiting harm to ecosystems. Developing new technologies, reducing resource use, and creating less waste are three ways to practice sustainability.

 What are sustainable practices?

Improving Resource Use

As you read in Chapter 2, many different interactions take place in ecosystems. Some organisms form close relationships with one other and their environment. Humans are like other organisms. We depend on the environment to help meet our requirements for life. Because many of the resources we rely on are limited, businesses and governments are changing the way they manage farms, forests, and energy resources. They are adopting sustainable practices.

Some farmers are practicing sustainable methods that protect land and provide nutritious food. Nearly one-third of U.S. farms practice conservation tillage, a method that involves planting seeds without plowing the soil. This technique can cut soil erosion by more than 90 percent. Organic farmers reject fertilizers and pesticides made from fossil fuels. Instead they use natural fertilizers, like compost, and natural pest controls, like ladybugs, which eat aphids.

Forestry practices are also changing. Cutting selectively instead of clear-cutting reduces soil erosion and encourages rapid regrowth. The U.S. Forest Service has adopted an ecosystem-management approach that tries to balance the need for timber with the need to conserve soil and water and preserve wildlife and biodiversity.

CHECK YOUR READING Give two examples of sustainable practices.

Energy companies are also promoting sustainability by developing alternative energy sources that do not come from fossil fuels. By the time you buy your first car, it may run on fuel cells, and the electricity in your house may be generated by a solar power plant.

Commercial geothermal power plants are a renewable energy source that uses the heat of molten rock in the Earth's interior. Geothermal power already supplies electricity to households in New Zealand, Japan, the United States, and elsewhere.

The energy of falling or flowing water can also be used to generate electricity in a hydropower plant. Commercial hydropower plants generate over half of the alternative energy used in the United States. Like solar and geothermal power, hydropower releases no pollutants. But hydropower often requires dams, which are expensive to build and can flood wildlife habitats and interfere with fish migration.

Wind is another source of energy that is clean and renewable. Large open areas with relatively constant winds are used as wind farms. Wind turbines are spread across these farms and convert the energy of moving air into electricity. Wind-generating capacity has increased steadily around the world in just the last ten years.

Solar Energy These mirrors collect and concentrate sunlight, which will be used to generate electricity.

INFER What benefits do people get from using mass transit? Why might some people be reluctant to use mass transit?

READING TiP

The prefix *re–* means *again*, so to *recycle* a resource is to use it again.

Reducing Waste and Pollution

Perhaps you are one of the many students who take a bus to school. Buses and trains are examples of mass transit, which move large groups of people at the same time. When you travel by mass transit, you are working to reduce waste and pollution. The photograph to the left shows a light rail train that carries commuters from downtown Portland, Oregon, into suburbs an hour away. In Portland, mass transit like this light rail helps reduce traffic congestion, air pollution, and noise pollution.

Another way to reduce pollution is by carpooling. Many states encourage carpools by reducing tolls or reserving highway lanes for cars carrying more than one person. Traffic is also reduced when workers telecommute, or work from home, using computers and telephones. Of course a telecommuter uses energy at home. But there are many ways to reduce home energy use. You can install compact fluorescent light bulbs, which use less electricity than a regular light bulb. And you can choose energy-efficient appliances.

 CHECK YOUR READING How does mass transit benefit the environment?

Most homes are heated with oil or natural gas, two nonrenewable resources. To use less of these resources, you lower your thermostat in winter or add insulation around doors and windows to keep heat inside. Many power companies offer a free energy audit, to show how you can use less energy at home.

Recycling is a fairly new idea in human communities, but if you think about it, it's what biological communities have always done to reduce waste and pollution. Resources are used again and again as they move through the water, nitrogen, and carbon cycles. Materials

These students are participating in a local recycling program.

that people now commonly recycle include glass, aluminum, certain types of plastic, office paper, newspaper, and cardboard.

Sometimes materials are recycled into the same product. Cans and glass bottles are melted down to make new cans and bottles. Materials can also be recycled into new products. Your warm fleece jacket might be made from recycled soda bottles. The cereal box on your breakfast table might be made from recycled paper.

 CHECK YOUR READING Name three things people can do at home that reduce waste and pollution.

Think globally, act locally.

Visitors to an ocean beach may find signs like the one on the right. Such signs remind people that small actions—like protecting the nests of sandpipers—make a difference in the preservation of ecosystems.

The challenges facing society are great. Providing Earth's growing population with clean water and air and with energy for warmth and transportation are only some of the many tasks. Scientists continue to learn about the interactions in ecosystems and how important ecosystems are to humans. As you have read about the interactions in ecosystems, you have probably realized that humans—including you—have a large effect on the natural world.

In the coming years, protection of ecosystems will remain a major challenge. By thinking globally, you will be able to understand the effects of society's decisions about resources, development, and transportation. By acting locally you can become involved in efforts to reduce the use of limited resources and to restore ecosystems.

BIRDS ONLY Beyond This Sign

3.3 Review

KEY CONCEPTS

1. List at least five ways that you can reduce your use of natural resources.

2. Describe three ways that resources can be managed in a sustainable way.

CRITICAL THINKING

3. **Infer** Controlling air and water pollution and protecting endangered species usually require the involvement of the federal government. Why can't state or local governments do this on their own?

○ CHALLENGE

4. **Apply** Explain how efforts to protect endangered species relate to restoration of ecosystems.

CHAPTER INVESTIGATION

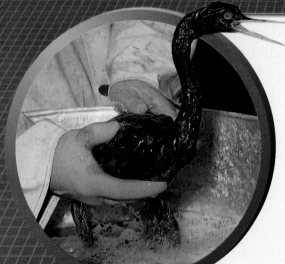

Cleaning Oil Spills

OVERVIEW AND PURPOSE

One example of a harmful effect of human activity is an oil spill. You've probably heard about oil spills in the news. Damage to an oil-carrying ship or barge can cause thick black oil to spill into the water. The oil floats on the water, and waves can carry the oil to shore. Oil gets caught on sand and living things that are part of a coastal ecosystem. These spills are especially difficult to clean up. In this investigation you will

- simulate an oil spill and test the effectiveness of various materials used to remove oil
- evaluate materials and processes used to clean up oil spills

▶ Problem

What materials are effective at removing oil spilled near a coastal ecosystem?

▶ Hypothesize

Write a hypothesis to propose a material or materials that might best remove oil from a coastal area. Your hypothesis should take the form of an "If . . . , then . . . , because . . ." statement.

▶ Procedure

1. Measure out 40 mL of vegetable oil in a small beaker. Stir in turmeric to make the oil yellow.

2. Pour sand into one end of the pan as shown to model a beach.

3. Carefully pour enough water into the pan so that it forms a model ocean at least 2 cm deep. Try not to disturb the sand pile.

4. Use the yellow-colored oil to model an oil spill. Pour the oil onto the slope of the sand so that it runs off into the water.

step 4

MATERIALS

- small beaker
- 40 mL vegetable oil
- turmeric
- spoon
- aluminum baking pan
- sand
- large beaker
- water
- sponge
- dish soap
- rubbing alcohol
- paper towels
- cotton balls
- cotton rag
- cornstarch
- yarn
- feather
- seaweed

Observe and Analyze

1. RECORD Write up your procedure for cleaning oil from sand and water. You may want to include a diagram.

2. EVALUATE What, if any, difficulties did you encounter in carrying out this experiment?

Conclude

1. INTERPRET How do your results compare with your hypothesis? Answer the problem statement.

2. EVALUATE Which materials were most useful for cleaning the water? Were they the same materials that were most useful for cleaning the sand?

3. EVALUATE Suppose you are trying to clean oil off of living things, such as a bird or seaweed. What process would you use?

4. IDENTIFY LIMITS In which ways did this demonstration fail to model a real oil spill?

INVESTIGATE Further

CHALLENGE Explain how the observations you made in this investigation might be useful in designing treatments for an actual oil spill.

5 Test the materials for effectiveness in removing the oil from the sand and the water.

6 Place the feather and the seaweed on the beach or in the water, where the oil is. Test materials for effectiveness in removing oil from the feather and seaweed.

7 Make a table in your **Science Notebook** like the one below. Record your observations on the effectiveness of each material.

8 Using your observations from step 7, design a process for removing oil from sand and water. This process may involve several materials and require a series of steps.

Cleaning Oil Spills

Problem What material or method is most effective in containing or cleaning up oil spills?

Hypothesis

Observations

	water	sand	feather	seaweed
paper towel				
cotton				

the BIG idea

Humans and human population growth affect the environment.

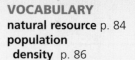
CONTENT REVIEW
CLASSZONE.COM

◀ KEY CONCEPTS SUMMARY

3.1 Human population growth presents challenges.

As the population continues to grow, there is a greater demand for natural resources. Cities and countries share many resources. Increasing populations put pressure on ecosystems.

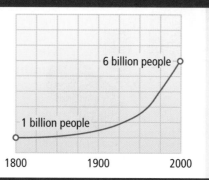

6 billion people

1 billion people

1800   1900   2000

VOCABULARY
natural resource p. 84
population density p. 86

3.2 Human activities affect the environment.

Pollution and habitat loss make it difficult for plants and animals to survive. Without the necessary resources, biodiversity of living things decreases, and ecosystems become less stable.

Pollution

Habitat Loss

VOCABULARY
pollution p. 91
biodiversity p. 91

3.3 Humans are working to protect ecosystems.

Working at local and governmental levels, humans are helping ecosystems recover.

Laws protect endangered species.

Researchers are investigating alternative resources.

VOCABULARY
conservation p. 99
sustainable p. 102

Reviewing Vocabulary

Place each vocabulary term at the center of a description wheel diagram. Write some words describing it on the spokes.

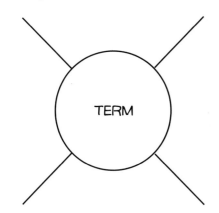

TERM

1. population density

2. natural resources

3. pollution

4. biodiversity

5. sustainable

6. conservation

Reviewing Key Concepts

Multiple Choice *Choose the letter of the best answer.*

7. In 2000, how big was Earth's human population?
   - **a.** 1 billion
   - **b.** 3 billion
   - **c.** 6 billion
   - **d.** 9 billion

8. Experts predict that by the year 2050, Earth's population will reach what number?
   - **a.** 3 billion
   - **b.** 6 billion
   - **c.** 9 billion
   - **d.** 12 billion

9. Which statement best explains why Earth's population has grown very rapidly in the last 100 years?
   - **a.** On average, women are having children at an older age.
   - **b.** People live longer because of improved health care and nutrition.
   - **c.** Global warming has enabled farmers to grow more food.
   - **d.** More land has been developed for housing.

10. Which of the four natural resources listed is likely to be used up the soonest?
    - **a.** petroleum
    - **b.** water
    - **c.** sunlight
    - **d.** wood

11. Which of the following is an example of increasing biodiversity?
    - **a.** A forest is clear-cut for its wood, leaving land available for new uses.
    - **b.** New species of animals and plants appear in a wildlife preserve.
    - **c.** A new species of plant outcompetes all of the others around a lake.
    - **d.** A cleared rain forest results in a change to a habitat.

12. Which represents a sustainable practice?
    - **a.** conservation tillage and use of natural fertilizers
    - **b.** more efficient removal of oil
    - **c.** allowing unlimited use of water for higher fees
    - **d.** restocking a lake with fish every year

13. What environmental problem does the Superfund Program address?
    - **a.** habitat loss
    - **b.** land development
    - **c.** biodiversity
    - **d.** pollution

Short Answer *Write a short answer to each question.*

14. List four ways increased human population density affects ecosystems.

15. Three ways that humans dispose of waste are landfills, incineration, and wastewater treatment plants. List one advantage and one disadvantage of each.

16. Write a paragraph to describe how an increase in population density affects land development.

Thinking Critically

Use the graph to answer the next three questions.

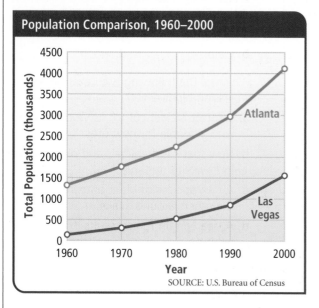

Population Comparison, 1960–2000

Total Population (thousands) vs. Year
SOURCE: U.S. Bureau of Census

17. COMPARE AND CONTRAST Describe the population size and rate of growth for the cities of Atlanta and Las Vegas. Would you expect the population of Las Vegas to ever get bigger than that of Atlanta based on the data supplied?

18. EVALUATE Is it possible to determine from the data shown whether the population density is higher in Atlanta than Las Vegas? What other information would you need?

19. CONNECT Atlanta is located in a temperate-forest biome and Las Vegas is located in a desert biome. How might the characteristics of these biomes affect the carrying capacity of the human populations in these cities?

20. PREDICT If states in the U.S. used less water from the Colorado River, how would the depth of the river in Mexico be affected?

21. COMPARE AND CONTRAST Explain why trees are generally considered a renewable resource. Now describe circumstances under which they could be considered a nonrenewable resource.

22. CLASSIFY Sort the resources below into the correct categories:

Resource	Renewable	Nonrenewable
Water		
Coal		
Soil		
Wood		
Copper		
Petroleum		
Aluminum		
Sunlight		

23. CALCULATE A compact fluorescent bulb uses less energy than a regular bulb. It is estimated that a coal-burning power plant would release 72 kilograms more carbon dioxide (CO_2) a year to power one regular bulb than it would to power one fluorescent bulb. If you replace five regular bulbs with five compact bulbs, how much less CO_2 would be released in a 10-year period?

the BIG idea

24. PROVIDE EXAMPLES Look again at the photograph on pages 78–79. How would you change or add details to your answer to the question on the photograph?

25. APPLY You are on the town council of a community located on a small island. The council has decided to make a brochure for the town's citizens. In your brochure, describe the island habitat. Include information about natural resources, such as water and soil. List the plants and animals that live there. Establish four rules that the community should follow to preserve the local habitat.

UNIT PROJECTS

Evaluate the materials in your project folder. Finish your project and get ready to present it to your class.

For practice on your
state test, go to . . .
TEST PRACTICE
CLASSZONE.COM

Standardized Test Practice

Analyzing Data

Nowhere is the impact of human population growth more obvious than in the growth of urbanized areas. Buildings, parking lots, and roads are replacing forests, farmland, and wetlands. The table below shows the growth of urbanized areas around 10 cities in the United States during a 20-year period.

1. What patterns can you see in the way information is presented from the top of the table to the bottom?

   a. Cities are arranged alphabetically.

   b. Cities are arranged by growth in population over 20 years.

   c. Cities are arranged by the growth in land area over 20 years.

   d. Cities are arranged by size of urban area.

2. How would you describe the change in the land around Atlanta between 1970 and 1990?

   a. In 1990, more land was used for farming.

   b. The number of buildings and roads increased.

   c. The urbanized area decreased.

   d. Natural habitats for birds increased.

3. Which type of graph would be best for displaying the data in the table?

   a. a bar graph

   b. a circle graph

   c. a line graph

   d. a double bar graph

4. How many square kilometers around Philadelphia were affected by urbanization between 1970 and 1990?

   a. 1116 km^2 **c.** 1068 km^2

   b. 1166 km^2 **d.** 1020 km^2

Growth in land area, 1970–1990

Location	Growth in Land Area (km^2)
Atlanta, GA	1816
Houston, TX	1654
New York City-N.E. New Jersey	1402
Washington, D.C.-MD-VA	1166
Philadelphia, PA	1068
Los Angeles, CA	1020
Dallas-Fort Worth, TX	964
Tampa-St. Petersburg-Clearwater, FL	929
Phoenix, AZ	916
Minneapolis-Saint Paul, MN	885

SOURCE: U.S. Bureau of Census data on Urbanized Areas

Extended Response

5. Write a paragraph to describe how a rural area would change if the land were developed and the area became more urban. Use the vocabulary words listed below in your answer.

population density	biodiversity
renewable resources	nonrenewable resources

6. If you were an urban designer working for a small city that expected to expand rapidly in the next 10 years, what recommendations would you make to the city council on how the land should be developed?

Student Resource Handbooks

Scientific Thinking Handbook

Making Observations

An **observation** is an act of noting and recording an event, characteristic, behavior, or anything else detected with an instrument or with the senses.

Observations allow you to make informed hypotheses and to gather data for experiments. Careful observations often lead to ideas for new experiments. There are two categories of observations:

- **Quantitative observations** can be expressed in numbers and include records of time, temperature, mass, distance, and volume.

- **Qualitative observations** include descriptions of sights, sounds, smells, and textures.

EXAMPLE

A student dissolved 30 grams of Epsom salts in water, poured the solution into a dish, and let the dish sit out uncovered overnight. The next day, she made the following observations of the Epsom salt crystals that grew in the dish.

To determine the mass, the student found the mass of the dish before and after growing the crystals and then used subtraction to find the difference.

The student measured several crystals and calculated the mean length. (To learn how to calculate the mean of a data set, see page R36.)

Table 1. Observations of Epsom Salt Crystals

Quantitative Observations	Qualitative Observations
• mass = 30 g • mean crystal length = 0.5 cm • longest crystal length = 2 cm	• Crystals are clear. • Crystals are long, thin, and rectangular. • White crust has formed around edge of dish.

Photographs or sketches are useful for recording qualitative observations.

Epsom salt crystals

MORE ABOUT OBSERVING

- Make quantitative observations whenever possible. That way, others will know exactly what you observed and be able to compare their results with yours.

- It is always a good idea to make qualitative observations too. You never know when you might observe something unexpected.

Predicting and Hypothesizing

A **prediction** is an expectation of what will be observed or what will happen. A **hypothesis** is a tentative explanation for an observation or scientific problem that can be tested by further investigation.

EXAMPLE

Suppose you have made two paper airplanes and you wonder why one of them tends to glide farther than the other one.

1. Start by asking a question.

2. Make an educated guess. After examination, you notice that the wings of the airplane that flies farther are slightly larger than the wings of the other airplane.

3. Write a prediction based upon your educated guess, in the form of an "If . . . , then . . ." statement. Write the independent variable after the word *if*, and the dependent variable after the word *then*.

4. To make a hypothesis, explain why you think what you predicted will occur. Write the explanation after the word *because*.

1. Why does one of the paper airplanes glide farther than the other?

2. The size of an airplane's wings may affect how far the airplane will glide.

3. Prediction: If I make a paper airplane with larger wings, then the airplane will glide farther.

> To read about independent and dependent variables, see page R30.

4. Hypothesis: If I make a paper airplane with larger wings, then the airplane will glide farther, because the additional surface area of the wing will produce more lift.

> Notice that the part of the hypothesis after *because* adds an explanation of why the airplane will glide farther.

MORE ABOUT HYPOTHESES

• The results of an experiment cannot prove that a hypothesis is correct. Rather, the results either support or do not support the hypothesis.

• Valuable information is gained even when your hypothesis is not supported by your results. For example, it would be an important discovery to find that wing size is not related to how far an airplane glides.

• In science, a hypothesis is supported only after many scientists have conducted many experiments and produced consistent results.

Inferring

An **inference** is a logical conclusion drawn from the available evidence and prior knowledge. Inferences are often made from observations.

EXAMPLE

A student observing a set of acorns noticed something unexpected about one of them. He noticed a white, soft-bodied insect eating its way out of the acorn.

The student recorded these observations.

Observations

- There is a hole in the acorn, about 0.5 cm in diameter, where the insect crawled out.
- There is a second hole, which is about the size of a pinhole, on the other side of the acorn.
- The inside of the acorn is hollow.

Here are some inferences that can be made on the basis of the observations.

Inferences

- The insect formed from the material inside the acorn, grew to its present size, and ate its way out of the acorn.
- The insect crawled through the smaller hole, ate the inside of the acorn, grew to its present size, and ate its way out of the acorn.
- An egg was laid in the acorn through the smaller hole. The egg hatched into a larva that ate the inside of the acorn, grew to its present size, and ate its way out of the acorn.

When you make inferences, be sure to look at all of the evidence available and combine it with what you already know.

MORE ABOUT INFERENCES

Inferences depend both on observations and on the knowledge of the people making the inferences. Ancient people who did not know that organisms are produced only by similar organisms might have made an inference like the first one. A student today might look at the same observations and make the second inference. A third student might have knowledge about this particular insect and know that it is never small enough to fit through the smaller hole, leading her to the third inference.

Identifying Cause and Effect

In a **cause-and-effect relationship,** one event or characteristic is the result of another. Usually an effect follows its cause in time.

There are many examples of cause-and-effect relationships in everyday life.

Cause	Effect
Turn off a light.	Room gets dark.
Drop a glass.	Glass breaks.
Blow a whistle.	Sound is heard.

Scientists must be careful not to infer a cause-and-effect relationship just because one event happens after another event. When one event occurs after another, you cannot infer a cause-and-effect relationship on the basis of that information alone. You also cannot conclude that one event caused another if there are alternative ways to explain the second event. A scientist must demonstrate through experimentation or continued observation that an event was truly caused by another event.

EXAMPLE

Make an Observation

Suppose you have a few plants growing outside. When the weather starts getting colder, you bring one of the plants indoors. You notice that the plant you brought indoors is growing faster than the others are growing. You cannot conclude from your observation that the change in temperature was the cause of the increased plant growth, because there are alternative explanations for the observation. Some possible explanations are given below.

- The humidity indoors caused the plant to grow faster.

- The level of sunlight indoors caused the plant to grow faster.

- The indoor plant's being noticed more often and watered more often than the outdoor plants caused it to grow faster.

- The plant that was brought indoors was healthier than the other plants to begin with.

To determine which of these factors, if any, caused the indoor plant to grow faster than the outdoor plants, you would need to design and conduct an experiment.

See pages R28–R35 for information about designing experiments.

Recognizing Bias

Television, newspapers, and the Internet are full of experts claiming to have scientific evidence to back up their claims. How do you know whether the claims are really backed up by good science?

SCIENTIFIC THINKING HANDBOOK

Bias is a slanted point of view, or personal prejudice. The goal of scientists is to be as objective as possible and to base their findings on facts instead of opinions. However, bias often affects the conclusions of researchers, and it is important to learn to recognize bias.

When scientific results are reported, you should consider the source of the information as well as the information itself. It is important to critically analyze the information that you see and read.

SOURCES OF BIAS

There are several ways in which a report of scientific information may be biased. Here are some questions that you can ask yourself:

1. **Who is sponsoring the research?**

   Sometimes, the results of an investigation are biased because an organization paying for the research is looking for a specific answer. This type of bias can affect how data are gathered and interpreted.

2. **Is the research sample large enough?**

   Sometimes research does not include enough data. The larger the sample size, the more likely that the results are accurate, assuming a truly random sample.

3. **In a survey, who is answering the questions?**

   The results of a survey or poll can be biased. The people taking part in the survey may have been specifically chosen because of how they would answer. They may have the same ideas or lifestyles. A survey or poll should make use of a random sample of people.

4. **Are the people who take part in a survey biased?**

   People who take part in surveys sometimes try to answer the questions the way they think the researcher wants them to answer. Also, in surveys or polls that ask for personal information, people may be unwilling to answer questions truthfully.

SCIENTIFIC BIAS

It is also important to realize that scientists have their own biases because of the types of research they do and because of their scientific viewpoints. Two scientists may look at the same set of data and come to completely different conclusions because of these biases. However, such disagreements are not necessarily bad. In fact, a critical analysis of disagreements is often responsible for moving science forward.

Identifying Faulty Reasoning

Faulty reasoning is wrong or incorrect thinking. It leads to mistakes and to wrong conclusions. Scientists are careful not to draw unreasonable conclusions from experimental data. Without such caution, the results of scientific investigations may be misleading.

EXAMPLE

Scientists try to make generalizations based on their data to explain as much about nature as possible. If only a small sample of data is looked at, however, a conclusion may be faulty. Suppose a scientist has studied the effects of the El Niño and La Niña weather patterns on flood damage in California from 1989 to 1995. The scientist organized the data in the bar graph below.

The scientist drew the following conclusions:

1. The La Niña weather pattern has no effect on flooding in California.
2. When neither weather pattern occurs, there is almost no flood damage.
3. A weak or moderate El Niño produces a small or moderate amount of flooding.
4. A strong El Niño produces a lot of flooding.

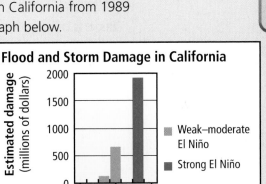

Flood and Storm Damage in California

SOURCE: *Governor's Office of Emergency Services, California*

For the six-year period of the scientist's investigation, these conclusions may seem to be reasonable. However, a six-year study of weather patterns may be too small of a sample for the conclusions to be supported. Consider the following graph, which shows information that was gathered from 1949 to 1997.

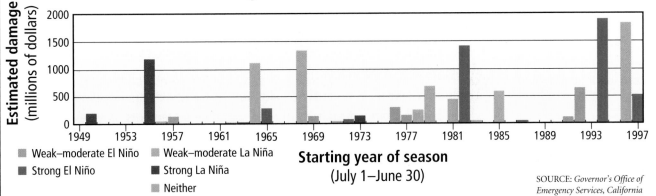

Flood and Storm Damage in California from 1949 to 1997

SOURCE: *Governor's Office of Emergency Services, California*

The only one of the conclusions that all of this information supports is number 3: a weak or moderate El Niño produces a small or moderate amount of flooding. By collecting more data, scientists can be more certain of their conclusions and can avoid faulty reasoning.

Analyzing Statements

To **analyze** a statement is to examine its parts carefully. Scientific findings are often reported through media such as television or the Internet. A report that is made public often focuses on only a small part of research. As a result, it is important to question the sources of information.

Evaluate Media Claims

To **evaluate** a statement is to judge it on the basis of criteria you've established. Sometimes evaluating means deciding whether a statement is true.

Reports of scientific research and findings in the media may be misleading or incomplete. When you are exposed to this information, you should ask yourself some questions so that you can make informed judgments about the information.

1. **Does the information come from a credible source?**

   Suppose you learn about a new product and it is stated that scientific evidence proves that the product works. A report from a respected news source may be more believable than an advertisement paid for by the product's manufacturer.

2. **How much evidence supports the claim?**

   Often, it may seem that there is new evidence every day of something in the world that either causes or cures an illness. However, information that is the result of several years of work by several different scientists is more credible than an advertisement that does not even cite the subjects of the experiment.

3. **How much information is being presented?**

   Science cannot solve all questions, and scientific experiments often have flaws. A report that discusses problems in a scientific study may be more believable than a report that addresses only positive experimental findings.

4. **Is scientific evidence being presented by a specific source?**

   Sometimes scientific findings are reported by people who are called experts or leaders in a scientific field. But if their names are not given or their scientific credentials are not reported, their statements may be less credible than those of recognized experts.

Differentiate Between Fact and Opinion

Sometimes information is presented as a fact when it may be an opinion. When scientific conclusions are reported, it is important to recognize whether they are based on solid evidence. Again, you may find it helpful to ask yourself some questions.

1. **What is the difference between a fact and an opinion?**

   A **fact** is a piece of information that can be strictly defined and proved true. An **opinion** is a statement that expresses a belief, value, or feeling. An opinion cannot be proved true or false. For example, a person's age is a fact, but if someone is asked how old they feel, it is impossible to prove the person's answer to be true or false.

2. **Can opinions be measured?**

   Yes, opinions can be measured. In fact, surveys often ask for people's opinions on a topic. But there is no way to know whether or not an opinion is the truth.

HOW TO DIFFERENTIATE FACT FROM OPINION

Human Activities and the Environment

Unfortunately, human use of fossil fuels is one of the most significant developments of the past few centuries. Humans rely on fossil fuels, a non-renewable energy resource, for more than 90 percent of their energy needs.

This careless misuse of our planet's resources has resulted in pollution, global warming, and the destruction of fragile ecosystems. For example, oil pipelines carry more than one million barrels of oil each day across tundra regions. Transporting oil across such areas can only result in oil spills that poison the land for decades.

Opinions

Notice words or phrases that express beliefs or feelings. The words *unfortunately* and *careless* show that opinions are being expressed.

Opinion

Look for statements that speculate about events. These statements are opinions, because they cannot be proved.

Facts

Statements that contain statistics tend to be facts. Writers often use facts to support their opinions.

Lab Handbook

Safety Rules

Before you work in the laboratory, read these safety rules twice. Ask your teacher to explain any rules that you do not completely understand. Refer to these rules later on if you have questions about safety in the science classroom.

Directions

- Read all directions and make sure that you understand them before starting an investigation or lab activity. If you do not understand how to do a procedure or how to use a piece of equipment, ask your teacher.
- Do not begin any investigation or touch any equipment until your teacher has told you to start.
- Never experiment on your own. If you want to try a procedure that the directions do not call for, ask your teacher for permission first.
- If you are hurt or injured in any way, tell your teacher immediately.

Dress Code

goggles

apron

gloves

- Wear goggles when
  — using glassware, sharp objects, or chemicals
  — heating an object
  — working with anything that can easily fly up into the air and hurt someone's eye
- Tie back long hair or hair that hangs in front of your eyes.
- Remove any article of clothing—such as a loose sweater or a scarf—that hangs down and may touch a flame, chemical, or piece of equipment.
- Observe all safety icons calling for the wearing of eye protection, gloves, and aprons.

Heating and Fire Safety

fire safety

heating safety

- Keep your work area neat, clean, and free of extra materials.
- Never reach over a flame or heat source.
- Point objects being heated away from you and others.
- Never heat a substance or an object in a closed container.
- Never touch an object that has been heated. If you are unsure whether something is hot, treat it as though it is. Use oven mitts, clamps, tongs, or a test-tube holder.
- Know where the fire extinguisher and fire blanket are kept in your classroom.
- Do not throw hot substances into the trash. Wait for them to cool or use the container your teacher puts out for disposal.

Electrical Safety

electrical safety

- Never use lamps or other electrical equipment with frayed cords.
- Make sure no cord is lying on the floor where someone can trip over it.
- Do not let a cord hang over the side of a counter or table so that the equipment can easily be pulled or knocked to the floor.
- Never let cords hang into sinks or other places where water can be found.
- Never try to fix electrical problems. Inform your teacher of any problems immediately.
- Unplug an electrical cord by pulling on the plug, not the cord.

Chemical Safety

chemical safety

poison

fumes

Wafting

- If you spill a chemical or get one on your skin or in your eyes, tell your teacher right away.
- Never touch, taste, or sniff any chemicals in the lab. If you need to determine odor, waft. Wafting consists of holding the chemical in its container 15 centimeters (6 in.) away from your nose, and using your fingers to bring fumes from the container to your nose.
- Keep lids on all chemicals you are not using.
- Never put unused chemicals back into the original containers. Throw away extra chemicals where your teacher tells you to.
- Pour chemicals over a sink or your work area, not over the floor.
- If you get a chemical in your eye, use the eyewash right away.
- Always wash your hands after handling chemicals, plants, or soil.

Glassware and Sharp-Object Safety

sharp objects

- If you break glassware, tell your teacher right away.
- Do not use broken or chipped glassware. Give these to your teacher.
- Use knives and other cutting instruments carefully. Always wear eye protection and cut away from you.

Animal Safety

- Never hurt an animal.
- Touch animals only when necessary. Follow your teacher's instructions for handling animals.
- Always wash your hands after working with animals.

Cleanup

disposal

- Follow your teacher's instructions for throwing away or putting away supplies.
- Clean your work area and pick up anything that has dropped to the floor.
- Wash your hands.

Using Lab Equipment

Different experiments require different types of equipment. But even though experiments differ, the ways in which the equipment is used are the same.

Beakers

- Use beakers for holding and pouring liquids.
- Do not use a beaker to measure the volume of a liquid. Use a graduated cylinder instead. (See page R16.)
- Use a beaker that holds about twice as much liquid as you need. For example, if you need 100 milliliters of water, you should use a 200- or 250-milliliter beaker.

Test Tubes

- Use test tubes to hold small amounts of substances.
- Do not use a test tube to measure the volume of a liquid.
- Use a test tube when heating a substance over a flame. Aim the mouth of the tube away from yourself and other people.
- Liquids easily spill or splash from test tubes, so it is important to use only small amounts of liquids.

Test-Tube Holder

- Use a test-tube holder when heating a substance in a test tube.
- Use a test-tube holder if the substance in a test tube is dangerous to touch.
- Make sure the test-tube holder tightly grips the test tube so that the test tube will not slide out of the holder.
- Make sure that the test-tube holder is above the surface of the substance in the test tube so that you can observe the substance.

Test-Tube Rack

- Use a test-tube rack to organize test tubes before, during, and after an experiment.

- Use a test-tube rack to keep test tubes upright so that they do not fall over and spill their contents.

- Use a test-tube rack that is the correct size for the test tubes that you are using. If the rack is too small, a test tube may become stuck. If the rack is too large, a test tube may lean over, and some of its contents may spill or splash.

Forceps

- Use forceps when you need to pick up or hold a very small object that should not be touched with your hands.

- Do not use forceps to hold anything over a flame, because forceps are not long enough to keep your hand safely away from the flame. Plastic forceps will melt, and metal forceps will conduct heat and burn your hand.

Hot Plate

- Use a hot plate when a substance needs to be kept warmer than room temperature for a long period of time.

- Use a hot plate instead of a Bunsen burner or a candle when you need to carefully control temperature.

- Do not use a hot plate when a substance needs to be burned in an experiment.

- Always use "hot hands" safety mitts or oven mitts when handling anything that has been heated on a hot plate.

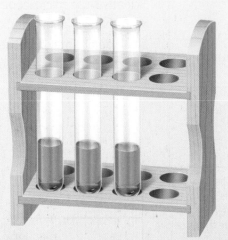

Microscope

Scientists use microscopes to see very small objects that cannot easily be seen with the eye alone. A microscope magnifies the image of an object so that small details may be observed. A microscope that you may use can magnify an object 400 times—the object will appear 400 times larger than its actual size.

Body The body separates the lens in the eyepiece from the objective lenses below.

Nosepiece The nosepiece holds the objective lenses above the stage and rotates so that all lenses may be used.

High-Power Objective Lens This is the largest lens on the nosepiece. It magnifies an image approximately 40 times.

Stage The stage supports the object being viewed.

Diaphragm The diaphragm is used to adjust the amount of light passing through the slide and into an objective lens.

Mirror or Light Source Some microscopes use light that is reflected through the stage by a mirror. Other microscopes have their own light sources.

Eyepiece Objects are viewed through the eyepiece. The eyepiece contains a lens that commonly magnifies an image 10 times.

Coarse Adjustment This knob is used to focus the image of an object when it is viewed through the low-power lens.

Fine Adjustment This knob is used to focus the image of an object when it is viewed through the high-power lens.

Low-Power Objective Lens This is the smallest lens on the nosepiece. It magnifies an image approximately 10 times.

Arm The arm supports the body above the stage. Always carry a microscope by the arm and base.

Stage Clip The stage clip holds a slide in place on the stage.

Base The base supports the microscope.

VIEWING AN OBJECT

1. Use the coarse adjustment knob to raise the body tube.

2. Adjust the diaphragm so that you can see a bright circle of light through the eyepiece.

3. Place the object or slide on the stage. Be sure that it is centered over the hole in the stage.

4. Turn the nosepiece to click the low-power lens into place.

5. Using the coarse adjustment knob, slowly lower the lens and focus on the specimen being viewed. Be sure not to touch the slide or object with the lens.

6. When switching from the low-power lens to the high-power lens, first raise the body tube with the coarse adjustment knob so that the high-power lens will not hit the slide.

7. Turn the nosepiece to click the high-power lens into place.

8. Use the fine adjustment knob to focus on the specimen being viewed. Again, be sure not to touch the slide or object with the lens.

MAKING A SLIDE, OR WET MOUNT

1. Place the specimen in the center of a clean slide.

2. Place a drop of water on the specimen.

3. Place a cover slip on the slide. Put one edge of the cover slip into the drop of water and slowly lower it over the specimen.

4. Remove any air bubbles from under the cover slip by gently tapping the cover slip.

5. Dry any excess water before placing the slide on the microscope stage for viewing.

Spring Scale (Force Meter)

- Use a spring scale to measure a force pulling on the scale.
- Use a spring scale to measure the force of gravity exerted on an object by Earth.
- To measure a force accurately, a spring scale must be zeroed before it is used. The scale is zeroed when no weight is attached and the indicator is positioned at zero.
- Do not attach a weight that is either too heavy or too light to a spring scale. A weight that is too heavy could break the scale or exert too great a force for the scale to measure. A weight that is too light may not exert enough force to be measured accurately.

Graduated Cylinder

- Use a graduated cylinder to measure the volume of a liquid.
- Be sure that the graduated cylinder is on a flat surface so that your measurement will be accurate.
- When reading the scale on a graduated cylinder, be sure to have your eyes at the level of the surface of the liquid.
- The surface of the liquid will be curved in the graduated cylinder. Read the volume of the liquid at the bottom of the curve, or meniscus (muh-NIHS-kuhs).
- You can use a graduated cylinder to find the volume of a solid object by measuring the increase in a liquid's level after you add the object to the cylinder.

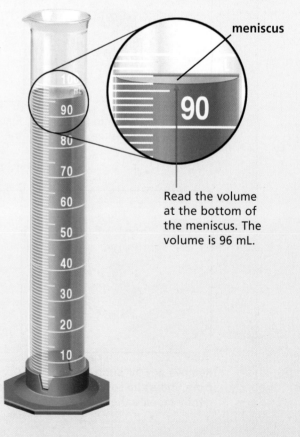

meniscus

Read the volume at the bottom of the meniscus. The volume is 96 mL.

Metric Rulers

- Use metric rulers or meter sticks to measure objects' lengths.

- Do not measure an object from the end of a metric ruler or meter stick, because the end is often imperfect. Instead, measure from the 1-centimeter mark, but remember to subtract a centimeter from the apparent measurement.

- Estimate any lengths that extend between marked units. For example, if a meter stick shows centimeters but not millimeters, you can estimate the length that an object extends between centimeter marks to measure it to the nearest millimeter.

- **Controlling Variables** If you are taking repeated measurements, always measure from the same point each time. For example, if you're measuring how high two different balls bounce when dropped from the same height, measure both bounces at the same point on the balls—either the top or the bottom. Do not measure at the top of one ball and the bottom of the other.

EXAMPLE

How to Measure a Leaf

1. Lay a ruler flat on top of the leaf so that the 1-centimeter mark lines up with one end. Make sure the ruler and the leaf do not move between the time you line them up and the time you take the measurement.

2. Look straight down on the ruler so that you can see exactly how the marks line up with the other end of the leaf.

3. Estimate the length by which the leaf extends beyond a marking. For example, the leaf below extends about halfway between the 4.2-centimeter and 4.3-centimeter marks, so the apparent measurement is about 4.25 centimeters.

4. Remember to subtract 1 centimeter from your apparent measurement, since you started at the 1-centimeter mark on the ruler and not at the end. The leaf is about 3.25 centimeters long (4.25 cm – 1 cm = 3.25 cm).

Triple-Beam Balance

This balance has a pan and three beams with sliding masses, called riders. At one end of the beams is a pointer that indicates whether the mass on the pan is equal to the masses shown on the beams.

1. Make sure the balance is zeroed before measuring the mass of an object. The balance is zeroed if the pointer is at zero when nothing is on the pan and the riders are at their zero points. Use the adjustment knob at the base of the balance to zero it.

2. Place the object to be measured on the pan.

3. Move the riders one notch at a time away from the pan. Begin with the largest rider. If moving the largest rider one notch brings the pointer below zero, begin measuring the mass of the object with the next smaller rider.

4. Change the positions of the riders until they balance the mass on the pan and the pointer is at zero. Then add the readings from the three beams to determine the mass of the object.

300 g	position of largest rider
90 g	position of middle rider
+ 3 g	position of smallest rider
393 g	mass of beaker

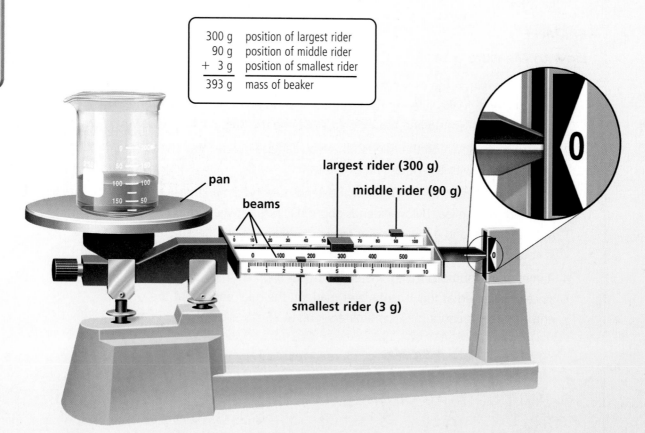

pan

beams

largest rider (300 g)

middle rider (90 g)

smallest rider (3 g)

Double-Pan Balance

This type of balance has two pans. Between the pans is a pointer that indicates whether the masses on the pans are equal.

1. Make sure the balance is zeroed before measuring the mass of an object. The balance is zeroed if the pointer is at zero when there is nothing on either of the pans. Many double-pan balances have sliding knobs that can be used to zero them.

2. Place the object to be measured on one of the pans.

3. Begin adding standard masses to the other pan. Begin with the largest standard mass. If this adds too much mass to the balance, begin measuring the mass of the object with the next smaller standard mass.

4. Add standard masses until the masses on both pans are balanced and the pointer is at zero. Then add the standard masses together to determine the mass of the object being measured.

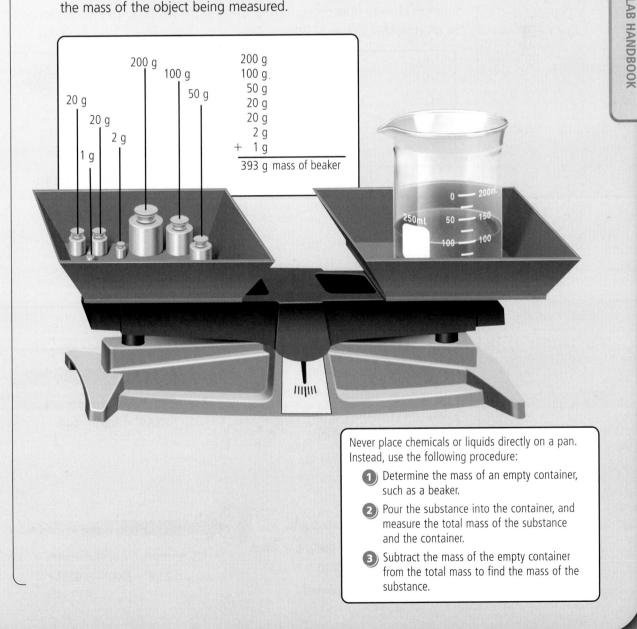

```
        200 g
              100 g        200 g
                    50 g   100 g
                            50 g
  20 g                      20 g
        20 g                20 g
              2 g            2 g
  1 g                    +   1 g
                         393 g mass of beaker
```

Never place chemicals or liquids directly on a pan. Instead, use the following procedure:

1. Determine the mass of an empty container, such as a beaker.

2. Pour the substance into the container, and measure the total mass of the substance and the container.

3. Subtract the mass of the empty container from the total mass to find the mass of the substance.

The Metric System and SI Units

Scientists use International System (SI) units for measurements of distance, volume, mass, and temperature. The International System is based on multiples of ten and the metric system of measurement.

Basic SI Units		
Property	**Name**	**Symbol**
length	meter	m
volume	liter	L
mass	kilogram	kg
temperature	kelvin	K

SI Prefixes		
Prefix	**Symbol**	**Multiple of 10**
kilo-	k	1000
hecto-	h	100
deca-	da	10
deci-	d	$0.1 \left(\frac{1}{10}\right)$
centi-	c	$0.01 \left(\frac{1}{100}\right)$
milli-	m	$0.001 \left(\frac{1}{1000}\right)$

Changing Metric Units

You can change from one unit to another in the metric system by multiplying or dividing by a power of 10.

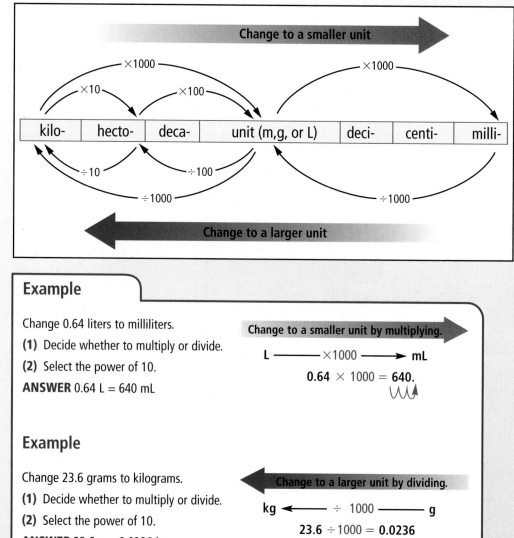

Example

Change 0.64 liters to milliliters.

(1) Decide whether to multiply or divide.

(2) Select the power of 10.

ANSWER 0.64 L = 640 mL

Change to a smaller unit by multiplying.

L ——— ×1000 ——→ mL

0.64 × 1000 = **640.**

Example

Change 23.6 grams to kilograms.

(1) Decide whether to multiply or divide.

(2) Select the power of 10.

ANSWER 23.6 g = 0.0236 kg

Change to a larger unit by dividing.

kg ←——— ÷ 1000 ——— g

23.6 ÷ 1000 = **0.0236**

LAB HANDBOOK

Temperature Conversions

Even though the kelvin is the SI base unit of temperature, the degree Celsius will be the unit you use most often in your science studies. The formulas below show the relationships between temperatures in degrees Fahrenheit (°F), degrees Celsius (°C), and kelvins (K).

$$°C = \frac{5}{9}(°F - 32)$$

$$°F = \frac{9}{5}°C + 32$$

$$K = °C + 273$$

See page R42 for help with using formulas.

See page R42 for help with using formulas.

Examples of Temperature Conversions

Condition	Degrees Celsius	Degrees Fahrenheit
Freezing point of water	0	32
Cool day	10	50
Mild day	20	68
Warm day	30	86
Normal body temperature	37	98.6
Very hot day	40	104
Boiling point of water	100	212

Converting Between SI and U.S. Customary Units

Use the chart below when you need to convert between SI units and U.S. customary units.

SI Unit	From SI to U.S. Customary			From U.S. Customary to SI		
Length	**When you know**	**multiply by**	**to find**	**When you know**	**multiply by**	**to find**
kilometer (km) = 1000 m	kilometers	0.62	miles	miles	1.61	kilometers
meter (m) = 100 cm	meters	3.28	feet	feet	0.3048	meters
centimeter (cm) = 10 mm	centimeters	0.39	inches	inches	2.54	centimeters
millimeter (mm) = 0.1 cm	millimeters	0.04	inches	inches	25.4	millimeters
Area	**When you know**	**multiply by**	**to find**	**When you know**	**multiply by**	**to find**
square kilometer (km^2)	square kilometers	0.39	square miles	square miles	2.59	square kilometers
square meter (m^2)	square meters	1.2	square yards	square yards	0.84	square meters
square centimeter (cm^2)	square centimeters	0.155	square inches	square inches	6.45	square centimeters
Volume	**When you know**	**multiply by**	**to find**	**When you know**	**multiply by**	**to find**
liter (L) = 1000 mL	liters	1.06	quarts	quarts	0.95	liters
	liters	0.26	gallons	gallons	3.79	liters
	liters	4.23	cups	cups	0.24	liters
	liters	2.12	pints	pints	0.47	liters
milliliter (mL) = 0.001 L	milliliters	0.20	teaspoons	teaspoons	4.93	milliliters
	milliliters	0.07	tablespoons	tablespoons	14.79	milliliters
	milliliters	0.03	fluid ounces	fluid ounces	29.57	milliliters
Mass	**When you know**	**multiply by**	**to find**	**When you know**	**multiply by**	**to find**
kilogram (kg) = 1000 g	kilograms	2.2	pounds	pounds	0.45	kilograms
gram (g) = 1000 mg	grams	0.035	ounces	ounces	28.35	grams

Precision and Accuracy

When you do an experiment, it is important that your methods, observations, and data be both precise and accurate.

low precision

precision, but not accuracy

precision and accuracy

Precision

In science, **precision** is the exactness and consistency of measurements. For example, measurements made with a ruler that has both centimeter and millimeter markings would be more precise than measurements made with a ruler that has only centimeter markings. Another indicator of precision is the care taken to make sure that methods and observations are as exact and consistent as possible. Every time a particular experiment is done, the same procedure should be used. Precision is necessary because experiments are repeated several times and if the procedure changes, the results will change.

EXAMPLE

Suppose you are measuring temperatures over a two-week period. Your precision will be greater if you measure each temperature at the same place, at the same time of day, and with the same thermometer than if you change any of these factors from one day to the next.

Accuracy

In science, it is possible to be precise but not accurate. **Accuracy** depends on the difference between a measurement and an actual value. The smaller the difference, the more accurate the measurement.

EXAMPLE

Suppose you look at a stream and estimate that it is about 1 meter wide at a particular place. You decide to check your estimate by measuring the stream with a meter stick, and you determine that the stream is 1.32 meters wide. However, because it is hard to measure the width of a stream with a meter stick, it turns out that you didn't do a very good job. The stream is actually 1.14 meters wide. Therefore, even though your estimate was less precise than your measurement, your estimate was actually more accurate.

Making Data Tables and Graphs

Data tables and graphs are useful tools for both recording and communicating scientific data.

Making Data Tables

You can use a **data table** to organize and record the measurements that you make. Some examples of information that might be recorded in data tables are frequencies, times, and amounts.

EXAMPLE

Suppose you are investigating photosynthesis in two elodea plants. One sits in direct sunlight, and the other sits in a dimly lit room. You measure the rate of photosynthesis by counting the number of bubbles in the jar every ten minutes.

1. Title and number your data table.
2. Decide how you will organize the table into columns and rows.
3. Any units, such as seconds or degrees, should be included in column headings, not in the individual cells.

Table 1. Number of Bubbles from Elodea

Time (min)	Sunlight	Dim Light
0	0	0
10	15	5
20	25	8
30	32	7
40	41	10
50	47	9
60	42	9

Always number and title data tables.

The data in the table above could also be organized in a different way.

Table 1. Number of Bubbles from Elodea

Light Condition	Time (min)						
	0	10	20	30	40	50	60
Sunlight	0	15	25	32	41	47	42
Dim light	0	5	8	7	10	9	9

Put units in column heading.

Making Line Graphs

You can use a **line graph** to show a relationship between variables. Line graphs are particularly useful for showing changes in variables over time.

EXAMPLE

Suppose you are interested in graphing temperature data that you collected over the course of a day.

Table 1. Outside Temperature During the Day on March 7

	Time of Day						
	7:00 A.M.	9:00 A.M.	11:00 A.M.	1:00 P.M.	3:00 P.M.	5:00 P.M.	7:00 P.M.
Temp (°C)	8	9	11	14	12	10	6

1. Use the vertical axis of your line graph for the variable that you are measuring—temperature.

2. Choose scales for both the horizontal axis and the vertical axis of the graph. You should have two points more than you need on the vertical axis, and the horizontal axis should be long enough for all of the data points to fit.

3. Draw and label each axis.

4. Graph each value. First find the appropriate point on the scale of the horizontal axis. Imagine a line that rises vertically from that place on the scale. Then find the corresponding value on the vertical axis, and imagine a line that moves horizontally from that value. The point where these two imaginary lines intersect is where the value should be plotted.

5. Connect the points with straight lines.

Be sure to add a number and a title to your graph.

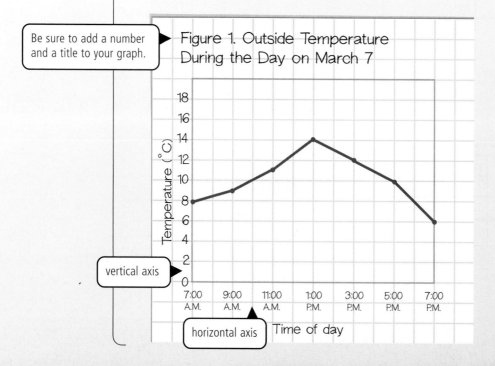

Figure 1. Outside Temperature During the Day on March 7

vertical axis

horizontal axis   Time of day

LAB HANDBOOK

Making Circle Graphs

You can use a **circle graph,** sometimes called a pie chart, to represent data as parts of a circle. Circle graphs are used only when the data can be expressed as percentages of a whole. The entire circle shown in a circle graph is equal to 100 percent of the data.

EXAMPLE

Suppose you identified the species of each mature tree growing in a small wooded area. You organized your data in a table, but you also want to show the data in a circle graph.

1. To begin, find the total number of mature trees.

   $56 + 34 + 22 + 10 + 28 = 150$

2. To find the degree measure for each sector of the circle, write a fraction comparing the number of each tree species with the total number of trees. Then multiply the fraction by 360°.

   Oak: $\frac{56}{150} \times 360° = 134.4°$

3. Draw a circle. Use a protractor to draw the angle for each sector of the graph.

4. Color and label each sector of the graph.

5. Give the graph a number and title.

Table 1. Tree Species in Wooded Area

Species	Number of Specimens
Oak	56
Maple	34
Birch	22
Willow	10
Pine	28

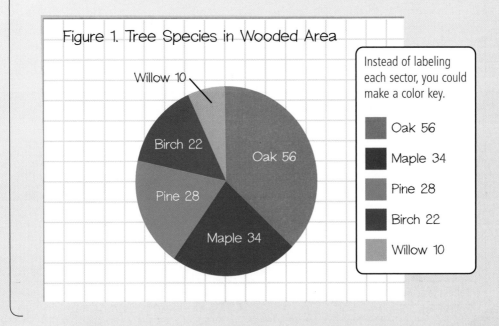

Figure 1. Tree Species in Wooded Area

Instead of labeling each sector, you could make a color key.

- Oak 56
- Maple 34
- Pine 28
- Birch 22
- Willow 10

Bar Graph

A **bar graph** is a type of graph in which the lengths of the bars are used to represent and compare data. A numerical scale is used to determine the lengths of the bars.

EXAMPLE

To determine the effect of water on seed sprouting, three cups were filled with sand, and ten seeds were planted in each. Different amounts of water were added to each cup over a three-day period.

Table 1. Effect of Water on Seed Sprouting

Daily Amount of Water (mL)	Number of Seeds That Sprouted After 3 Days in Sand
0	1
10	4
20	8

1. Choose a numerical scale. The greatest value is 8, so the end of the scale should have a value greater than 8, such as 10. Use equal increments along the scale, such as increments of 2.

2. Draw and label the axes. Mark intervals on the vertical axis according to the scale you chose.

3. Draw a bar for each data value. Use the scale to decide how long to make each bar.

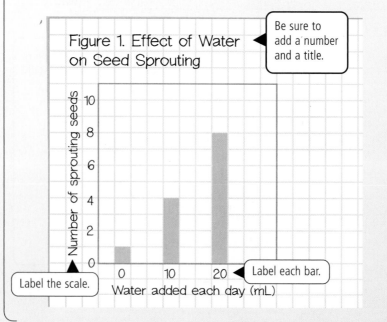

Figure 1. Effect of Water on Seed Sprouting

Be sure to add a number and a title.

Label the scale.

Label each bar.

Double Bar Graph

A **double bar graph** is a bar graph that shows two sets of data. The two bars for each measurement are drawn next to each other.

EXAMPLE

The seed-sprouting experiment was done using both sand and potting soil. The data for sand and potting soil can be plotted on one graph.

1. Draw one set of bars, using the data for sand, as shown below.
2. Draw bars for the potting-soil data next to the bars for the sand data. Shade them a different color. Add a key.

Table 2. Effect of Water and Soil on Seed Sprouting

Daily Amount of Water (mL)	Number of Seeds That Sprouted After 3 Days in Sand	Number of Seeds That Sprouted After 3 Days in Potting Soil
0	1	2
10	4	5
20	8	9

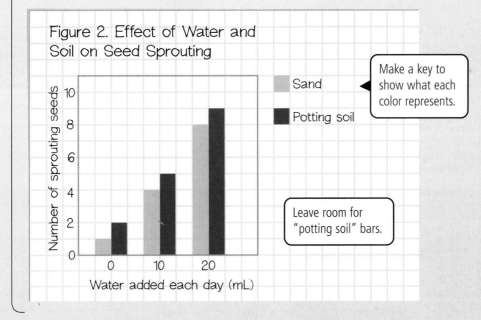

Figure 2. Effect of Water and Soil on Seed Sprouting

Make a key to show what each color represents.

Leave room for "potting soil" bars.

Designing an Experiment

Use this section when designing or conducting an experiment.

Determining a Purpose

You can find a purpose for an experiment by doing research, by examining the results of a previous experiment, or by observing the world around you. An **experiment** is an organized procedure to study something under controlled conditions.

> Don't forget to learn as much as possible about your topic before you begin.

1. Write the purpose of your experiment as a question or problem that you want to investigate.

2. Write down research questions and begin searching for information that will help you design an experiment. Consult the library, the Internet, and other people as you conduct your research.

EXAMPLE

Middle school students observed an odor near the lake by their school. They also noticed that the water on the side of the lake near the school was greener than the water on the other side of the lake. The students did some research to learn more about their observations. They discovered that the odor and green color in the lake

came from algae. They also discovered that a new fertilizer was being used on a field nearby. The students inferred that the use of the fertilizer might be related to the presence of the algae and designed a controlled experiment to find out whether they were right.

Problem

How does fertilizer affect the presence of algae in a lake?

Research Questions

- Have other experiments been done on this problem? If so, what did those experiments show?
- What kind of fertilizer is used on the field? How much?
- How do algae grow?
- How do people measure algae?
- Can fertilizer and algae be used safely in a lab? How?

> **Research**
> As you research, you may find a topic that is more interesting to you than your original topic, or learn that a procedure you wanted to use is not practical or safe. It is OK to change your purpose as you research.

Writing a Hypothesis

A **hypothesis** is a tentative explanation for an observation or scientific problem that can be tested by further investigation. You can write your hypothesis in the form of an "If . . . , then . . . , because . . ." statement.

Hypothesis

If the amount of fertilizer in lake water is increased, then the amount of algae will also increase, because fertilizers provide nutrients that algae need to grow.

Hypotheses
For help with hypotheses, refer to page R3.

Determining Materials

Make a list of all the materials you will need to do your experiment. Be specific, especially if someone else is helping you obtain the materials. Try to think of everything you will need.

Materials

- 1 large jar or container
- 4 identical smaller containers
- rubber gloves that also cover the arms
- sample of fertilizer-and-water solution
- eyedropper
- clear plastic wrap
- scissors
- masking tape
- marker
- ruler

Determining Variables and Constants

EXPERIMENTAL GROUP AND CONTROL GROUP

An experiment to determine how two factors are related always has two groups—a control group and an experimental group.

1. Design an experimental group. Include as many trials as possible in the experimental group in order to obtain reliable results.

2. Design a control group that is the same as the experimental group in every way possible, except for the factor you wish to test.

Experimental Group: two containers of lake water with one drop of fertilizer solution added to each

Control Group: two containers of lake water with no fertilizer solution added

Go back to your materials list and make sure you have enough items listed to cover both your experimental group and your control group.

VARIABLES AND CONSTANTS

Identify the variables and constants in your experiment. In a controlled experiment, a **variable** is any factor that can change. **Constants** are all of the factors that are the same in both the experimental group and the control group.

1. Read your hypothesis. The **independent variable** is the factor that you wish to test and that is manipulated or changed so that it can be tested. The independent variable is expressed in your hypothesis after the word *if*. Identify the independent variable in your laboratory report.

2. The **dependent variable** is the factor that you measure to gather results. It is expressed in your hypothesis after the word *then*. Identify the dependent variable in your laboratory report.

Hypothesis
If the amount of fertilizer in lake water is increased, then the amount of algae will also increase, because fertilizers provide nutrients that algae need to grow.

Table 1. Variables and Constants in Algae Experiment

Independent Variable	Dependent Variable	Constants
Amount of fertilizer in lake water	Amount of algae that grow	• Where the lake water is obtained • Type of container used • Light and temperature conditions where water will be stored

Set up your experiment so that you will test only one variable.

LAB HANDBOOK

MEASURING THE DEPENDENT VARIABLE

Before starting your experiment, you need to define how you will measure the dependent variable. An **operational definition** is a description of the one particular way in which you will measure the dependent variable.

Your operational definition is important for several reasons. First, in any experiment there are several ways in which a dependent variable can be measured. Second, the procedure of the experiment depends on how you decide to measure the dependent variable. Third, your operational definition makes it possible for other people to evaluate and build on your experiment.

EXAMPLE 1

An operational definition of a dependent variable can be qualitative. That is, your measurement of the dependent variable can simply be an observation of whether a change occurs as a result of a change in the independent variable. This type of operational definition can be thought of as a "yes or no" measurement.

Table 2. Qualitative Operational Definition of Algae Growth

Independent Variable	Dependent Variable	Operational Definition
Amount of fertilizer in lake water	Amount of algae that grow	Algae grow in lake water

A qualitative measurement of a dependent variable is often easy to make and record. However, this type of information does not provide a great deal of detail in your experimental results.

EXAMPLE 2

An operational definition of a dependent variable can be quantitative. That is, your measurement of the dependent variable can be a number that shows how much change occurs as a result of a change in the independent variable.

Table 3. Quantitative Operational Definition of Algae Growth

Independent Variable	Dependent Variable	Operational Definition
Amount of fertilizer in lake water	Amount of algae that grow	Diameter of largest algal growth (in mm)

A quantitative measurement of a dependent variable can be more difficult to make and analyze than a qualitative measurement. However, this type of data provides much more information about your experiment and is often more useful.

Writing a Procedure

Write each step of your procedure. Start each step with a verb, or action word, and keep the steps short. Your procedure should be clear enough for someone else to use as instructions for repeating your experiment.

If necessary, go back to your materials list and add any materials that you left out.

Controlling Variables
The same amount of fertilizer solution must be added to two of the four containers.

Controlling Variables
All four containers must receive the same amount of light.

Procedure

1. Put on your gloves. Use the large container to obtain a sample of lake water.

2. Divide the sample of lake water equally among the four smaller containers.

3. Use the eyedropper to add one drop of fertilizer solution to two of the containers.

4. Use the masking tape and the marker to label the containers with your initials, the date, and the identifiers "Jar 1 with Fertilizer," "Jar 2 with Fertilizer," "Jar 1 without Fertilizer," and "Jar 2 without Fertilizer."

5. Cover the containers with clear plastic wrap. Use the scissors to punch ten holes in each of the covers.

6. Place all four containers on a window ledge. Make sure that they all receive the same amount of light.

7. Observe the containers every day for one week.

8. Use the ruler to measure the diameter of the largest clump of algae in each container, and record your measurements daily.

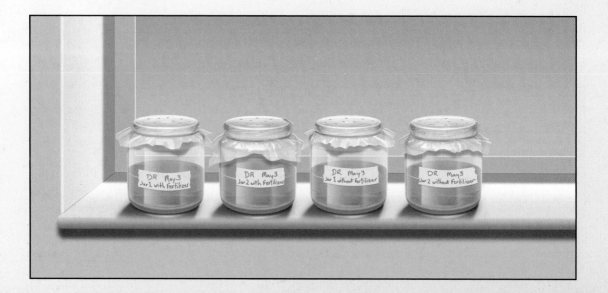

Recording Observations

Once you have obtained all of your materials and your procedure has been approved, you can begin making experimental observations. Gather both quantitative and qualitative data. If something goes wrong during your procedure, make sure you record that too.

> **Observations**
> For help with making qualitative and quantitative observations, refer to page R2.

> For more examples of data tables, see page R23.

Table 4. Fertilizer and Algae Growth

Date and Time	Experimental Group		Control Group		Observations
	Jar 1 with Fertilizer (diameter of algae in mm)	Jar 2 with Fertilizer (diameter of algae in mm)	Jar 1 without Fertilizer (diameter of algae in mm)	Jar 2 without Fertilizer (diameter of algae in mm)	
5/3 4:00 P.M.	0	0	0	0	condensation in all containers
5/4 4:00 P.M.	0	3	0	0	tiny green blobs in jar 2 with fertilizer
5/5 4:15 P.M.	4	5	0	3	green blobs in jars 1 and 2 with fertilizer and jar 2 without fertilizer
5/6 4:00 P.M.	5	6	0	4	water light green in jar 2 with fertilizer
5/7 4:00 P.M.	8	10	0	6	water light green in jars 1 and 2 with fertilizer and in jar 2 without fertilizer
5/8 3:30 P.M.	10	18	0	6	cover off jar 2 with fertilizer
5/9 3:30 P.M.	14	23	0	8	drew sketches of each container

> Notice that on the sixth day, the observer found that the cover was off one of the containers. It is important to record observations of unintended factors because they might affect the results of the experiment.

> Use technology, such as a microscope, to help you make observations when possible.

Drawings of Samples Viewed Under Microscope on 5/9 at 100x

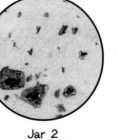

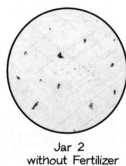

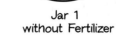

| Jar 1 with Fertilizer | Jar 2 with Fertilizer | Jar 1 without Fertilizer | Jar 2 without Fertilizer |

Summarizing Results

To summarize your data, look at all of your observations together. Look for meaningful ways to present your observations. For example, you might average your data or make a graph to look for patterns. When possible, use spreadsheet software to help you analyze and present your data. The two graphs below show the same data.

EXAMPLE 1

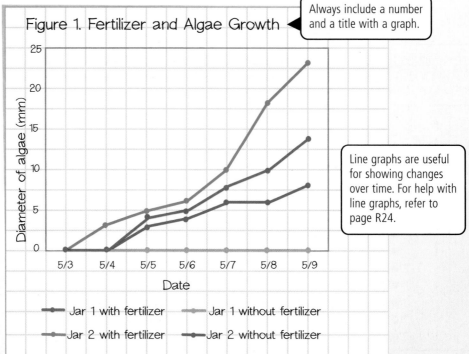

> Always include a number and a title with a graph.

> Line graphs are useful for showing changes over time. For help with line graphs, refer to page R24.

EXAMPLE 2

> Bar graphs are useful for comparing different data sets. This bar graph has four bars for each day. Another way to present the data would be to calculate averages for the tests and the controls, and to show one test bar and one control bar for each day.

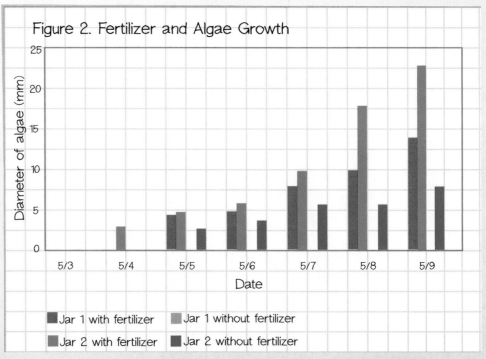

Drawing Conclusions

RESULTS AND INFERENCES

To draw conclusions from your experiment, first write your results. Then compare your results with your hypothesis. Do your results support your hypothesis? Be careful not to make inferences about factors that you did not test.

> For help with making inferences, see page R4.

Results and Inferences

The results of my experiment show that more algae grew in lake water to which fertilizer had been added than in lake water to which no fertilizer had been added. My hypothesis was supported. I infer that it is possible that the growth of algae in the lake was caused by the fertilizer used on the field.

> Notice that you cannot conclude from this experiment that the presence of algae in the lake was due only to the fertilizer.

QUESTIONS FOR FURTHER RESEARCH

Write a list of questions for further research and investigation. Your ideas may lead you to new experiments and discoveries.

Questions for Further Research

- What is the connection between the amount of fertilizer and algae growth?
- How do different brands of fertilizer affect algae growth?
- How would algae growth in the lake be affected if no fertilizer were used on the field?
- How do algae affect the lake and the other life in and around it?
- How does fertilizer affect the lake and the life in and around it?
- If fertilizer is getting into the lake, how is it getting there?

Math Handbook

Describing a Set of Data

Means, medians, modes, and ranges are important math tools for describing data sets such as the following widths of fossilized clamshells.

13 mm   25 mm   14 mm   21 mm   16 mm   23 mm   14 mm

Mean

The **mean** of a data set is the sum of the values divided by the number of values.

Example

To find the mean of the clamshell data, add the values and then divide the sum by the number of values.

$$\frac{13 \text{ mm} + 25 \text{ mm} + 14 \text{ mm} + 21 \text{ mm} + 16 \text{ mm} + 23 \text{ mm} + 14 \text{ mm}}{7} = \frac{126 \text{ mm}}{7} = 18 \text{ mm}$$

ANSWER The mean is 18 mm.

Median

The **median** of a data set is the middle value when the values are written in numerical order. If a data set has an even number of values, the median is the mean of the two middle values.

Example

To find the median of the clamshell data, arrange the values in order from least to greatest. The median is the middle value.

13 mm   14 mm   14 mm   16 mm   21 mm   23 mm   25 mm

ANSWER The median is 16 mm.

Mode

The **mode** of a data set is the value that occurs most often.

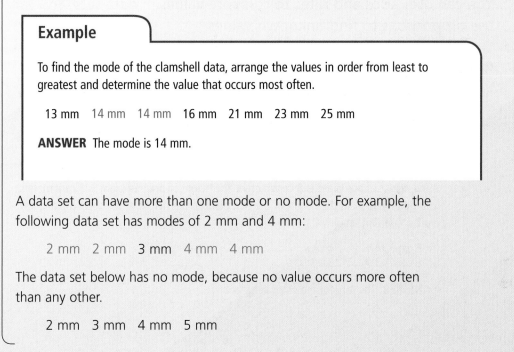

Example

To find the mode of the clamshell data, arrange the values in order from least to greatest and determine the value that occurs most often.

  13 mm   14 mm   14 mm   16 mm   21 mm   23 mm   25 mm

ANSWER The mode is 14 mm.

A data set can have more than one mode or no mode. For example, the following data set has modes of 2 mm and 4 mm:

  2 mm   2 mm   3 mm   4 mm   4 mm

The data set below has no mode, because no value occurs more often than any other.

  2 mm   3 mm   4 mm   5 mm

Range

The **range** of a data set is the difference between the greatest value and the least value.

Example

To find the range of the clamshell data, arrange the values in order from least to greatest.

  13 mm   14 mm   14 mm   16 mm   21 mm   23 mm   25 mm

Subtract the least value from the greatest value.

  13 mm is the least value.
  25 mm is the greatest value.

  25 mm − 13 mm = 12 mm

ANSWER The range is 12 mm.

Using Ratios, Rates, and Proportions

You can use ratios and rates to compare values in data sets. You can use proportions to find unknown values.

Ratios

A **ratio** uses division to compare two values. The ratio of a value a to a nonzero value b can be written as $\frac{a}{b}$.

Example

The height of one plant is 8 centimeters. The height of another plant is 6 centimeters. To find the ratio of the height of the first plant to the height of the second plant, write a fraction and simplify it.

$$\frac{8\text{ cm}}{6\text{ cm}} = \frac{4 \times \overset{1}{\cancel{2}}}{3 \times \underset{1}{\cancel{2}}} = \frac{4}{3}$$

ANSWER The ratio of the plant heights is $\frac{4}{3}$.

You can also write the ratio $\frac{a}{b}$ as "a to b" or as $a:b$. For example, you can write the ratio of the plant heights as "4 to 3" or as $4:3$.

Rates

A **rate** is a ratio of two values expressed in different units. A unit rate is a rate with a denominator of 1 unit.

Example

A plant grew 6 centimeters in 2 days. The plant's rate of growth was $\frac{6\text{ cm}}{2\text{ days}}$. To describe the plant's growth in centimeters per day, write a unit rate.

Divide numerator and denominator by 2: $\quad \frac{6\text{ cm}}{2\text{ days}} = \frac{6\text{ cm} \div 2}{2\text{ days} \div 2}$

You divide 2 days by 2 to get 1 day, so divide 6 cm by 2 also.

Simplify: $\quad = \frac{3\text{ cm}}{1\text{ day}}$

ANSWER The plant's rate of growth is 3 centimeters per day.

Proportions

A **proportion** is an equation stating that two ratios are equivalent. To solve for an unknown value in a proportion, you can use cross products.

Example

If a plant grew 6 centimeters in 2 days, how many centimeters would it grow in 3 days (if its rate of growth is constant)?

$$\textit{Write a proportion:} \quad \frac{6 \text{ cm}}{2 \text{ days}} = \frac{x}{3 \text{ days}}$$

$$\textit{Set cross products:} \quad 6 \text{ cm} \cdot 3 = 2x$$

$$\textit{Multiply 6 and 3:} \quad 18 \text{ cm} = 2x$$

$$\textit{Divide each side by 2:} \quad \frac{18 \text{ cm}}{2} = \frac{2x}{2}$$

$$\textit{Simplify:} \quad 9 \text{ cm} = x$$

ANSWER The plant would grow 9 centimeters in 3 days.

Using Decimals, Fractions, and Percents

Decimals, fractions, and percentages are all ways of recording and representing data.

Decimals

A **decimal** is a number that is written in the base-ten place value system, in which a decimal point separates the ones and tenths digits. The values of each place is ten times that of the place to its right.

Example

A caterpillar traveled from point A to point C along the path shown.

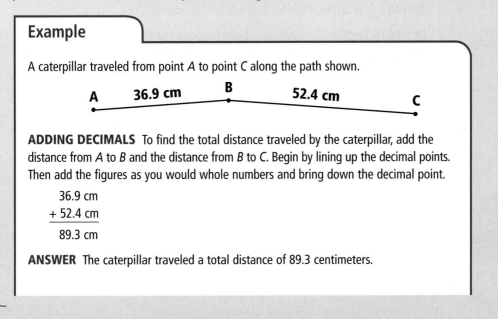

ADDING DECIMALS To find the total distance traveled by the caterpillar, add the distance from A to B and the distance from B to C. Begin by lining up the decimal points. Then add the figures as you would whole numbers and bring down the decimal point.

$$\begin{array}{r} 36.9 \text{ cm} \\ + 52.4 \text{ cm} \\ \hline 89.3 \text{ cm} \end{array}$$

ANSWER The caterpillar traveled a total distance of 89.3 centimeters.

Example continued

SUBTRACTING DECIMALS To find how much farther the caterpillar traveled on the second leg of the journey, subtract the distance from *A* to *B* from the distance from *B* to *C*.

$$\begin{array}{r} 52.4 \text{ cm} \\ - \ 36.9 \text{ cm} \\ \hline 15.5 \text{ cm} \end{array}$$

ANSWER The caterpillar traveled 15.5 centimeters farther on the second leg of the journey.

Example

A caterpillar is traveling from point *D* to point *F* along the path shown. The caterpillar travels at a speed of 9.6 centimeters per minute.

MULTIPLYING DECIMALS You can multiply decimals as you would whole numbers. The number of decimal places in the product is equal to the sum of the number of decimal places in the factors.

For instance, suppose it takes the caterpillar 1.5 minutes to go from *D* to *E*. To find the distance from *D* to *E*, multiply the caterpillar's speed by the time it took.

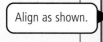

Align as shown.

$$\begin{array}{r} 9.6 \\ \times \ 1.5 \\ \hline 480 \\ 96 \ \ \\ \hline 14.40 \end{array}$$
$$\begin{array}{l} 1 \quad \text{decimal place} \\ + 1 \quad \text{decimal place} \\ \\ \\ \\ 2 \quad \text{decimal places} \end{array}$$

ANSWER The distance from *D* to *E* is 14.4 centimeters.

DIVIDING DECIMALS When you divide by a decimal, move the decimal points the same number of places in the divisor and the dividend to make the divisor a whole number.

For instance, to find the time it will take the caterpillar to travel from *E* to *F*, divide the distance from *E* to *F* by the caterpillar's speed.

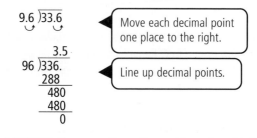

Move each decimal point one place to the right.

Line up decimal points.

ANSWER The caterpillar will travel from *E* to *F* in 3.5 minutes.

MATH HANDBOOK

Fractions

A **fraction** is a number in the form $\frac{a}{b}$, where b is not equal to 0. A fraction is in **simplest form** if its numerator and denominator have a greatest common factor (GCF) of 1. To simplify a fraction, divide its numerator and denominator by their GCF.

Example

A caterpillar is 40 millimeters long. The head of the caterpillar is 6 millimeters long. To compare the length of the caterpillar's head with the caterpillar's total length, you can write and simplify a fraction that expresses the ratio of the two lengths.

Write the ratio of the two lengths: $\dfrac{\text{Length of head}}{\text{Total length}} = \dfrac{6 \text{ mm}}{40 \text{ mm}}$

Write numerator and denominator as products of numbers and the GCF: $= \dfrac{3 \times 2}{20 \times 2}$

Divide numerator and denominator by the GCF: $= \dfrac{3 \times \overset{1}{\cancel{2}}}{20 \times \underset{1}{\cancel{2}}}$

Simplify: $= \dfrac{3}{20}$

ANSWER In simplest form, the ratio of the lengths is $\dfrac{3}{20}$.

Percents

A **percent** is a ratio that compares a number to 100. The word *percent* means "per hundred" or "out of 100." The symbol for *percent* is %.

For instance, suppose 43 out of 100 caterpillars are female. You can represent this ratio as a percent, a decimal, or a fraction.

Percent	Decimal	Fraction
43%	0.43	$\dfrac{43}{100}$

Example

In the preceding example, the ratio of the length of the caterpillar's head to the caterpillar's total length is $\dfrac{3}{20}$. To write this ratio as a percent, write an equivalent fraction that has a denominator of 100.

Multiply numerator and denominator by 5: $\dfrac{3}{20} = \dfrac{3 \times 5}{20 \times 5}$

$= \dfrac{15}{100}$

Write as a percent: $= 15\%$

ANSWER The caterpillar's head represents 15 percent of its total length.

Using Formulas

A **formula** is an equation that shows the general relationship between two or more quantities.

In science, a formula often has a word form and a symbolic form. The formula below expresses Ohm's law.

Word Form

$$Current = \frac{voltage}{resistance}$$

Symbolic Form

$$I = \frac{V}{R}$$

In this formula, I, V, and R are variables. A mathematical **variable** is a symbol or letter that is used to represent one or more numbers.

> The term *variable* is also used in science to refer to a factor that can change during an experiment.

Example

Suppose that you measure a voltage of 1.5 volts and a resistance of 15 ohms. You can use the formula for Ohm's law to find the current in amperes.

Write the formula for Ohm's law: $\quad I = \dfrac{V}{R}$

Substitute 1.5 volts for V and 15 ohms for R: $\quad I = \dfrac{1.5 \text{ volts}}{15 \text{ ohms}}$

Simplify: $\quad I = 0.1 \text{ amp}$

ANSWER The current is 0.1 ampere.

If you know the values of all variables but one in a formula, you can solve for the value of the unknown variable. For instance, Ohm's law can be used to find a voltage if you know the current and the resistance.

Example

Suppose that you know that a current is 0.2 amperes and the resistance is 18 ohms. Use the formula for Ohm's law to find the voltage in volts.

Write the formula for Ohm's law: $\quad I = \dfrac{V}{R}$

Substitute 0.2 amp for I and 18 ohms for R: $\quad 0.2 \text{ amp} = \dfrac{V}{18 \text{ ohms}}$

Multiply both sides by 18 ohms: $\quad 0.2 \text{ amp} \cdot 18 \text{ ohms} = V$

Simplify: $\quad 3.6 \text{ volts} = V$

ANSWER The voltage is 3.6 volts.

Finding Areas

The area of a figure is the amount of surface the figure covers.

Area is measured in square units, such as square meters (m^2) or square centimeters (cm^2). Formulas for the areas of three common geometric figures are shown below.

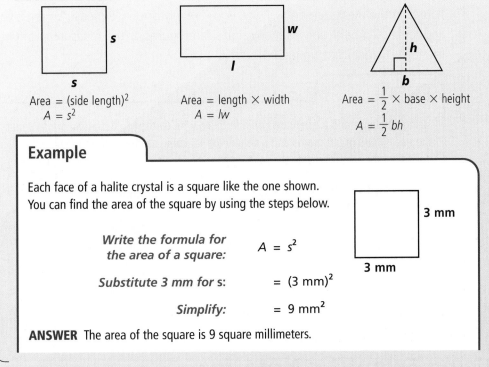

Area = (side length)^2
$A = s^2$

Area = length × width
$A = lw$

Area = $\frac{1}{2}$ × base × height
$A = \frac{1}{2} bh$

Example

Each face of a halite crystal is a square like the one shown. You can find the area of the square by using the steps below.

3 mm

3 mm

Write the formula for the area of a square:	$A = s^2$
Substitute 3 mm for s:	$= (3 \text{ mm})^2$
Simplify:	$= 9 \text{ mm}^2$

ANSWER The area of the square is 9 square millimeters.

MATH HANDBOOK

Finding Volumes

The volume of a solid is the amount of space contained by the solid.

Volume is measured in cubic units, such as cubic meters (m^3) or cubic centimeters (cm^3). The volume of a rectangular prism is given by the formula shown below.

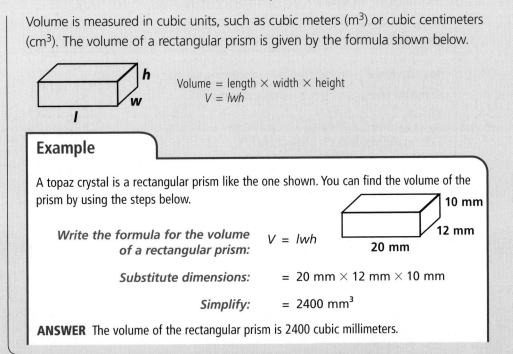

Volume = length × width × height
$V = lwh$

Example

A topaz crystal is a rectangular prism like the one shown. You can find the volume of the prism by using the steps below.

10 mm

12 mm

20 mm

Write the formula for the volume of a rectangular prism:	$V = lwh$
Substitute dimensions:	$= 20 \text{ mm} \times 12 \text{ mm} \times 10 \text{ mm}$
Simplify:	$= 2400 \text{ mm}^3$

ANSWER The volume of the rectangular prism is 2400 cubic millimeters.

Using Significant Figures

The **significant figures** in a decimal are the digits that are warranted by the accuracy of a measuring device.

When you perform a calculation with measurements, the number of significant figures to include in the result depends in part on the number of significant figures in the measurements. When you multiply or divide measurements, your answer should have only as many significant figures as the measurement with the fewest significant figures.

Example

Using a balance and a graduated cylinder filled with water, you determined that a marble has a mass of 8.0 grams and a volume of 3.5 cubic centimeters. To calculate the density of the marble, divide the mass by the volume.

Write the formula for density: Density $= \dfrac{\text{mass}}{\text{Volume}}$

Substitute measurements: $= \dfrac{8.0 \text{ g}}{3.5 \text{ cm}^3}$

Use a calculator to divide: ≈ 2.285714286 g/cm^3

ANSWER Because the mass and the volume have two significant figures each, give the density to two significant figures. The marble has a density of 2.3 grams per cubic centimeter.

Using Scientific Notation

Scientific notation is a shorthand way to write very large or very small numbers. For example, 73,500,000,000,000,000,000,000 kg is the mass of the Moon. In scientific notation, it is 7.35×10^{22} kg.

Example

You can convert from standard form to scientific notation.

Standard Form	Scientific Notation
720,000	7.2×10^5
5 decimal places left	Exponent is 5.
0.000291	2.91×10^{-4}
4 decimal places right	Exponent is −4.

You can convert from scientific notation to standard form.

Scientific Notation	Standard Form
4.63×10^7	46,300,000
Exponent is 7.	7 decimal places right
1.08×10^{-6}	0.00000108
Exponent is −6.	6 decimal places left

Note-Taking Handbook

Note-Taking Strategies

Taking notes as you read helps you understand the information. The notes you take can also be used as a study guide for later review. This handbook presents several ways to organize your notes.

Content Frame

1. Make a chart in which each column represents a category.
2. Give each column a heading.
3. Write details under the headings.

NAME	GROUP	CHARACTERISTICS	DRAWING
snail	mollusks	mantle, shell	
ant	arthropods	six legs, exoskeleton	
earthworm	segmented worms	segmented body, circulatory and digestive systems	
heartworm	roundworms	digestive system	
sea star	echinoderms	spiny skin, tube feet	
jellyfish	cnidarians	stinging cells	

categories

details

Combination Notes

1. For each new idea or concept, write an informal outline of the information.
2. Make a sketch to illustrate the concept, and label it.

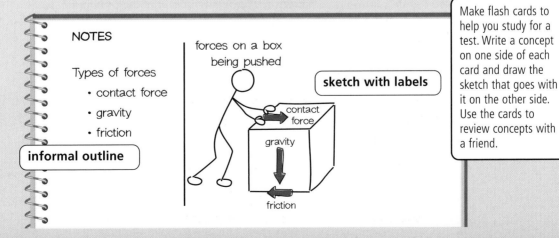

NOTES

Types of forces
- contact force
- gravity
- friction

informal outline

forces on a box being pushed

sketch with labels

contact force

gravity

friction

Make flash cards to help you study for a test. Write a concept on one side of each card and draw the sketch that goes with it on the other side. Use the cards to review concepts with a friend.

Main Idea and Detail Notes

1. In the left-hand column of a two-column chart, list main ideas. The blue headings express main ideas throughout this textbook.

2. In the right-hand column, write details that expand on each main idea.

You can shorten the headings in your chart. Be sure to use the most important words.

When studying for tests, cover up the detail notes column with a sheet of paper. Then use each main idea to form a question—such as "How does latitude affect climate?" Answer the question, and then uncover the detail notes column to check your answer.

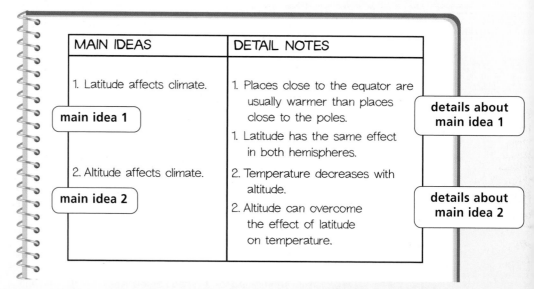

MAIN IDEAS	DETAIL NOTES
1. Latitude affects climate. — main idea 1	1. Places close to the equator are usually warmer than places close to the poles. 1. Latitude has the same effect in both hemispheres. — details about main idea 1
2. Altitude affects climate. — main idea 2	2. Temperature decreases with altitude. 2. Altitude can overcome the effect of latitude on temperature. — details about main idea 2

Main Idea Web

1. Write a main idea in a box.

2. Add boxes around it with related vocabulary terms and important details.

You can find definitions near highlighted terms.

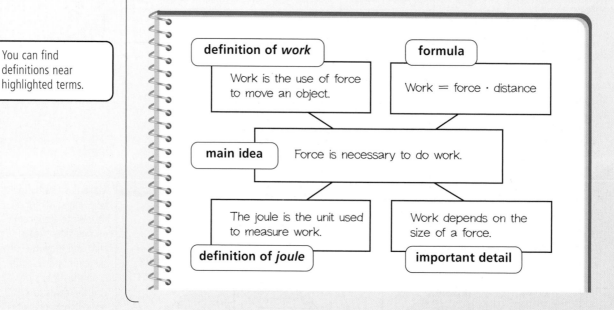

definition of *work*
Work is the use of force to move an object.

formula
Work = force · distance

main idea
Force is necessary to do work.

The joule is the unit used to measure work.
definition of *joule*

Work depends on the size of a force.
important detail

Mind Map

1. Write a main idea in the center.

2. Add details that relate to one another and to the main idea.

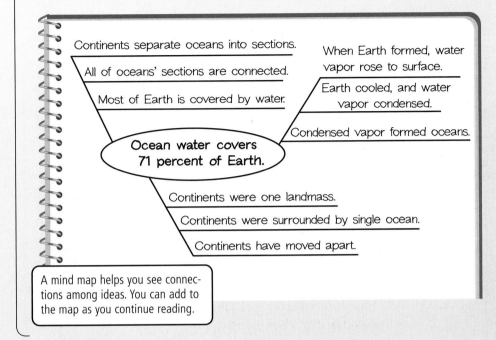

Continents separate oceans into sections.

All of oceans' sections are connected.

Most of Earth is covered by water.

When Earth formed, water vapor rose to surface.

Earth cooled, and water vapor condensed.

Condensed vapor formed oceans.

Ocean water covers 71 percent of Earth.

Continents were one landmass.

Continents were surrounded by single ocean.

Continents have moved apart.

A mind map helps you see connections among ideas. You can add to the map as you continue reading.

Supporting Main Ideas

1. Write a main idea in a box.

2. Add boxes underneath with information—such as reasons, explanations, and examples—that supports the main idea.

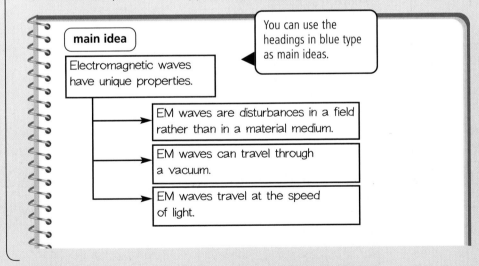

main idea

Electromagnetic waves have unique properties.

You can use the headings in blue type as main ideas.

EM waves are disturbances in a field rather than in a material medium.

EM waves can travel through a vacuum.

EM waves travel at the speed of light.

Outline

1. Copy the chapter title and headings from the book in the form of an outline.

2. Add notes that summarize in your own words what you read.

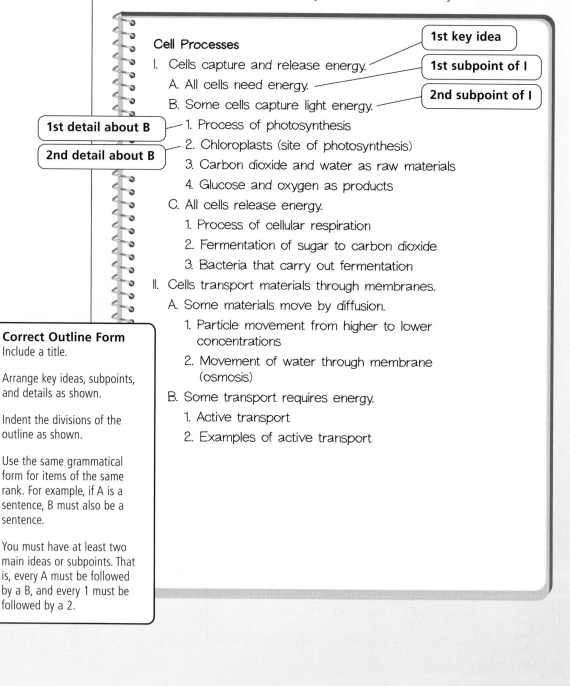

Cell Processes

1st key idea

I. Cells capture and release energy.

1st subpoint of I

A. All cells need energy.

2nd subpoint of I

B. Some cells capture light energy.

1st detail about B
1. Process of photosynthesis

2nd detail about B
2. Chloroplasts (site of photosynthesis)
3. Carbon dioxide and water as raw materials
4. Glucose and oxygen as products

C. All cells release energy.
1. Process of cellular respiration
2. Fermentation of sugar to carbon dioxide
3. Bacteria that carry out fermentation

II. Cells transport materials through membranes.

A. Some materials move by diffusion.
1. Particle movement from higher to lower concentrations
2. Movement of water through membrane (osmosis)

B. Some transport requires energy.
1. Active transport
2. Examples of active transport

Correct Outline Form

Include a title.

Arrange key ideas, subpoints, and details as shown.

Indent the divisions of the outline as shown.

Use the same grammatical form for items of the same rank. For example, if A is a sentence, B must also be a sentence.

You must have at least two main ideas or subpoints. That is, every A must be followed by a B, and every 1 must be followed by a 2.

NOTE-TAKING HANDBOOK

Concept Map

1. Write an important concept in a large oval.
2. Add details related to the concept in smaller ovals.
3. Write linking words on arrows that connect the ovals.

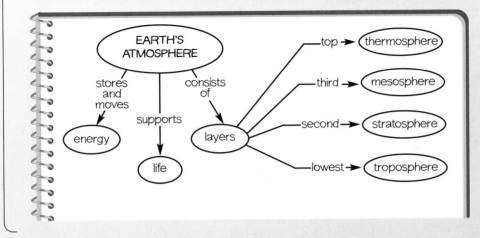

The main ideas or concepts can often be found in the blue headings. An example is "The atmosphere stores and moves energy." Use nouns from these concepts in the ovals, and use the verb or verbs on the lines.

Venn Diagram

1. Draw two overlapping circles, one for each item that you are comparing.
2. In the overlapping section, list the characteristics that are shared by both items.
3. In the outer sections, list the characteristics that are peculiar to each item.
4. Write a summary that describes the information in the Venn diagram.

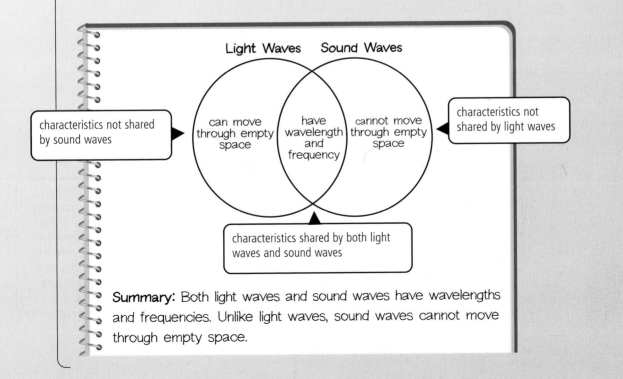

Summary: Both light waves and sound waves have wavelengths and frequencies. Unlike light waves, sound waves cannot move through empty space.

Vocabulary Strategies

Important terms are highlighted in this book. A definition of each term can be found in the sentence or paragraph where the term appears. You can also find definitions in the Glossary. Taking notes about vocabulary terms helps you understand and remember what you read.

Description Wheel

1. Write a term inside a circle.
2. Write words that describe the term on "spokes" attached to the circle.

When studying for a test with a friend, read the phrases on the spokes one at a time until your friend identifies the correct term.

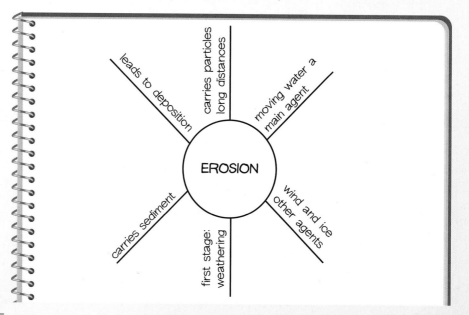

Four Square

1. Write a term in the center.
2. Write details in the four areas around the term.

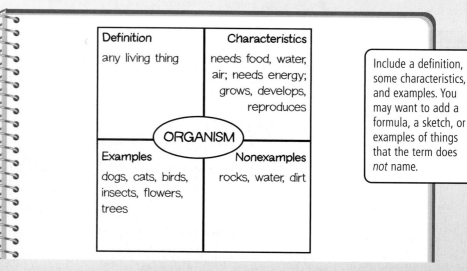

Include a definition, some characteristics, and examples. You may want to add a formula, a sketch, or examples of things that the term does *not* name.

NOTE-TAKING HANDBOOK

Frame Game

1. Write a term in the center.
2. Frame the term with details.

Include examples, descriptions, sketches, or sentences that use the term in context. Change the frame to fit each new term.

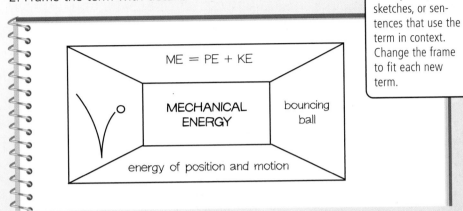

Magnet Word

1. Write a term on the magnet.
2. On the lines, add details related to the term.

You can also use phrases or sentences on the lines.

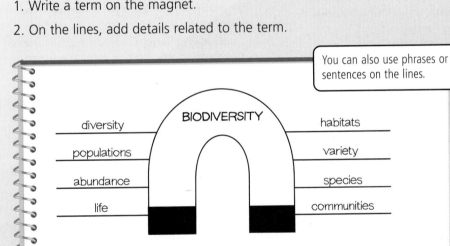

Word Triangle

1. Write a term and its definition in the bottom section.
2. In the middle section, write a sentence in which the term is used correctly.
3. In the top section, draw a small picture to illustrate the term.

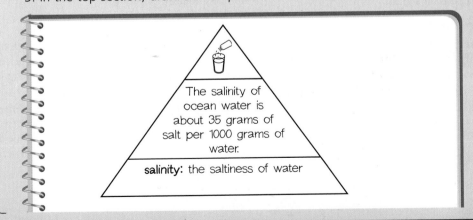

Glossary

A

abiotic factor (AY-by-AHT-ihk)
A nonliving physical or chemical part of an ecosystem. (p. 10)

> **factor abiótico** Una parte física o química sin vida de un ecosistema.

adaptation
A characteristic, a behavior, or any inherited trait that makes a species able to survive and reproduce in a particular environment. (p. xxi)

> **adaptación** Una característica, un comportamiento o cualquier rasgo heredado que permite a una especie sobrevivir o reproducirse en un medio ambiente determinado.

atom
The smallest particle of an element that has the chemical properties of that element.

> **átomo** La partícula más pequeña de un elemento que tiene las propiedades químicas de ese elemento.

B

biodiversity
The number and variety of living things found on Earth or within an ecosystem. (p. 91)

> **biodiversidad** La cantidad y variedad de organismos vivos que se encuentran en la Tierra o dentro de un ecosistema.

biology
The scientific study of life and all living things; ecology, zoology, and botany are examples of biological sciences.

> **biología** El estudio científico de la vida y de todos los organismos vivos; la ecología, la zoología y la botántica son ejemplos de ciencias biológicas.

biome (BY-OHM)
A region of Earth that has a particular climate and certain types of plants. Examples are tundra, taiga, desert, grassland, temperate and tropical forests. (p. 30)

> **bioma** Una región de la Tierra que tiene un clima particular y ciertos tipos de plantas. La tundra, la taiga, el desierto, la estepa, la selva tropical y el bosque templado son ejemplos de biomas.

C

biotic factor (by-AHT-ihk)
A living thing in an ecosystem. (p. 10)

> **factor biótico** Un organismo vivo en un ecosistema.

carbon cycle
The continuous movement of carbon through Earth, its atmosphere, and the living things on Earth. (p. 18)

> **ciclo del carbono** El movimiento continuo del carbono en la Tierra, su atmósfera y todos los seres vivos en ella.

carrying capacity
The maximum size that a population can reach in an ecosystem. (p. 65)

> **capacidad de carga** El tamaño máximo que una población puede alcanzar en un ecosistema.

cell
The smallest unit that is able to perform the basic functions of life. (p. xv)

> **célula** La unidad más pequeña capaz de realizar las funciones básicas de la vida.

classification
The systematic grouping of different types of organisms by their shared characteristics.

> **clasificación** La agrupación sistemática de diferentes tipos de organismos en base a las características que comparten.

commensalism (kuh-MEHN-suh-LIHZ-uhm)
An interaction between two species in which one species benefits without harming the other; a type of symbiosis. (p. 59)

> **comensalismo** Una interacción entre dos especies en la cual una especie se beneficia sin causar daño a la otra; un tipo de simbiosis.

community
All the populations that live and interact with each other in a particular place. The community can live in a place as small as a pond or a park, or it can live in a place as large as a rain forest or the ocean. (p. 48)

> **comunidad** Todas las poblaciones que viven e interactúan entre sí en un lugar. La comunidad puede vivir en un lugar tan pequeño como una laguna o un parque o en un lugar tan grande como un bosque tropical o el océano.

competition

The struggle between two or more living things that depend on the same limited resource. (p. 55)

competencia La lucha entre dos o más organismos vivos que dependen del mismo recurso limitado.

compound

A substance made up of two or more different types of atoms bonded together.

compuesto Una sustancia formada por dos o más diferentes tipos de átomos enlazados.

coniferous (koh-NIHF-uhr-uhs)

A term used to describe cone-bearing trees and shrubs that usually keep their leaves or needles during all the seasons of the year; examples are pine, fir, and spruce trees. (p. 32)

conífero Un término usado para describir a los árboles y los arbustos que producen conos o piñas y que generalmente conservan sus hojas o agujas durante todas las estaciones del año; el pino, el abeto y la picea son ejemplos de coníferas.

conservation

The process of saving or protecting a natural resource. (p. 99)

conservación El proceso de salvar o proteger un recurso natural.

consumer

A living thing that gets its energy by eating other living things in a food chain; consumers are also called heterotrophs. (p. 24)

consumidor Un organismo vivo que obtiene su energía alimentándose de oros organismos vivos en una cadena alimentaria; los consumidores también son llamados heterótrofos.

cooperation

A term used to describe an interaction between two or more living things in which they are said to work together. (p. 57)

cooperación Un término que describe la interacción entre dos o más organismos vivos en la cual se dice que trabajan juntos.

cycle

n. A series of events or actions that repeat themselves regularly; a physical and/or chemical process in which one material continually changes locations and/or forms. Examples include the water cycle, the carbon cycle, and the rock cycle. (p. 16)

v. To move through a repeating series of events or actions.

ciclo Una serie de eventos o acciones que se repiten regularmente; un proceso físico y/o químico en el cual un material cambia continuamente de lugar y/o forma. Ejemplos: el ciclo del agua, el ciclo del carbono y el ciclo de las rocas.

D

data

Information gathered by observation or experimentation that can be used in calculating or reasoning. *Data* is a plural word; the singular is *datum.*

datos Información reunida mediante observación o experimentación y que se puede usar para calcular o para razonar.

deciduous (dih-SIHJ-oo-uhs)

A term used to describe trees and shrubs that drop their leaves when winter comes; examples are maple, oak, and birch trees. (p. 33)

caducifolio Un término usado para describir árboles y arbustos que dejan caer sus hojas cuando llega el invierno; el arce, el roble y el abedul son ejemplos de árboles caducifolios.

decomposer

An organism that feeds on and breaks down dead plant or animal matter. (p. 25)

organismo descomponedor Un organismo que se alimenta de y degrada materia vegetal o animal.

density

A property of matter representing the mass per unit volume.

densidad Una propiedad de la materia que representa la masa por unidad de volumen.

diversity

A term used to describe the quality of having many differences; *biodiversity* describes the great variety and many differences found among living things.

diversidad Un término usado para describir la cualidad de tener muchas diferencias; la biodiversidad describe la gran variedad y las muchas diferencias encontradas entre organismos vivos.

DNA

The genetic material found in all living cells that contains the information needed for an organism to grow, maintain itself, and reproduce. Deoxyribonucleic acid (dee-AHK-see-RY-boh-noo-KLEE-ihk).

ADN El material genético que se encuentra en todas las céulas vivas y que contiene la información necesaria para que un organismo crezca, se mantenga a sí mismo y se reproduzca. Ácido desoxiribunucleico.

E

ecology

The scientific study of how living things interact with each other and their environment. (p. 9)

ecología El estudio científico de cómo interactúan los organismos vivos entre sí y con su medio ambiente.

ecosystem

All the living and nonliving things that interact in a particular environment. An ecosystem can be as small as a meadow or a swamp or as large as a forest or a desert. (p. 9)

ecosistema Todos los organismos vivos y las cosas que interactúan en un medio ambiente específico. Un ecosistema puede ser tan pequeño como un prado o un pantano, o tan grande como un bosque o un desierto.

element

A substance that cannot be broken down into a simpler substance by ordinary chemical changes. An element consists of atoms of only one type.

elemento Una sustancia que no puede descomponerse en otra sustancia más simple por medio de cambios químicos normales. Un elemento consta de átomos de un solo tipo.

energy

The ability to do work or to cause a change. For example, the energy of a moving bowling ball knocks over pins; energy from food allows animals to move and to grow; and energy from the Sun heats Earth's surface and atmosphere, which causes air to move.

energía La capacidad para trabajar o causar un cambio. Por ejemplo, la energía de una bola de boliche en movimiento tumba los pinos; la energía proveniente de su alimento permite a los animales moverse y crecer; la energía del Sol calienta la superficie y la atmósfera de la Tierra, lo que ocasiona que el aire se mueva.

energy pyramid

A model used to show the amount of energy available to living things in an ecosystem. (p. 28)

pirámide de energía Un modelo usado para mostrar la cantidad de energía disponible para organismos vivos en un ecosistema.

environment

Everything that surrounds a living thing. An environment is made up of both living and nonliving factors. (p. xix)

medio ambiente Todo lo que rodea a un organismo vivo. Un medio ambiente está compuesto de factores vivos y factores sin vida.

estuary

The lower end of a river where it meets the ocean and fresh and salt waters mix. (p. 36)

estuario La parte baja de un río donde desemboca en el océano y donde el agua dulce del río se mezcla con el agua salada del mar.

experiment

An organized procedure to study something under controlled conditions. (p. xxiv)

experimento Un procedimiento organizado para estudiar algo bajo condiciones controladas.

extinction

The permanent disappearance of a species. (p. xxi)

extinción La desaparición permanente de una especie.

F

food chain

A model used to show the feeding relationship between a single producer and a chain of consumers in an ecosystem. In a typical food chain, a plant is the producer that is eaten by a consumer, such as an insect; then the insect is eaten by a second consumer, such as a bird. (p. 26)

cadena alimentaria Un modelo usado para mostrar la relación de ingestión entre un solo productor y una cadena de consumidores en un ecosistema. En una cadena alimentaria típica, una planta es la productora que es ingerida por un consumidor como un insecto, y luego el insecto es ingerido por un segundo consumidor como un pájaro.

food web

A model used to show a feeding relationship in which many food chains overlap in an ecosystem. (p. 26)

red trófica Un modelo usado para mostrar una relación de consumo en la cual muchas cadenas alimentarias se empalman en un ecosistema.

G

genetic material

The nucleic acid DNA that is present in all living cells and contains the information needed for a cell's growth, maintenance, and reproduction.

material genético El ácido nucleico ADN, ue esta presente en todas las células vivas y que contiene la información necesaria para el crecimiento, el mantenimiento y la reproducción celular.

H

habitat

The natural environment in which a living thing gets all that it needs to live; examples include a desert, a coral reef, and a freshwater lake. (p. 46)

hábitat El medio ambiente natural en el cual un organismo vivo consigue todo lo que requiere para vivir; ejemplos incluyen un desierto, un arrecife coralino y un lago de agua dulce.

hypothesis

A tentative explanation for an observation or phenomenon. A hypothesis is used to make testable predictions. (p. xxiv)

hipótesis Una explicación provisional de una observación o de un fenómeno. Una hipótesis se usa para hacer predicciones que se pueden probar.

I, J, K

interaction
The condition of acting or having an influence upon something. Living things in an ecosystem interact with both the living and nonliving parts of their environment. (p. xix)

interacción La condición de actuar o influir sobre algo. Los organismos vivos en un ecosistema interactúan con las partes vivas y las partes sin vida de su medio ambiente.

L

law
In science, a rule or principle describing a physical relationship that always works in the same way under the same conditions. The law of conservation of energy is an example.

ley En las ciencias, una regla o un principio que describe una relación física que siempre funciona de la misma manera bajo las mismas condiciones. La ley de la conservación de la energía es un ejemplo.

limiting factor
A factor or condition that prevents the continuing growth of a population in an ecosystem. (p. 64)

factor limitante Un factor o una condición que impide el crecimiento continuo de una población en un ecosistema.

M

mass
A measure of how much matter an object is made of.

masa Una medida de la cantidad de materia de la que está compuesto un objeto.

matter
Anything that has mass and volume. Matter exists ordinarily as a solid, a liquid, or a gas.

materia Todo lo que tiene masa y volumen. Generalmente la materia existe como sólido, líquido o gas.

molecule
A group of atoms that are held together by covalent bonds so that they move as a single unit.

molécula Un grupo de átomos que están unidos mediante enlaces covalentes de tal manera que se mueven como una sola unidad.

mutualism (MYOO-choo-uh-LIHZ-uhm)
An interaction between two species in which both benefit; a type of symbiosis. (p. 58)

mutualismo Una interacción entre dos especies en la cual ambas se benefician; un tipo de simbiosis.

N

natural resource
Any type of matter or energy from Earth's environment that humans use to meet their needs. (p. 84)

recurso natural Cualquier tipo de materia o energía del medio ambiente de la Tierra que usan los humanos para satisfacer sus necesidades.

niche (nihch)
The role a living thing plays in its habitat. A plant is a food producer, whereas an insect both consumes food as well as provides food for other consumers. (p. 47)

nicho El papel que juega un organismo vivo en su hábitat. Una planta es un productor de alimento mientras que un insecto consume alimento y a la vez sirve de alimento a otros consumidores.

nitrogen cycle
The continuous movement of nitrogen through Earth, its atmosphere, and the living things on Earth. (p. 19)

ciclo del nitrógeno El movimiento continuo de nitrógeno por la Tierra, su atmósfera y los organismos vivos de la Tierra.

nutrient (NOO-tree-uhnt)
A substance that an organism needs to live. Examples include water, minerals, and materials that come from the breakdown of food particles.

nutriente Una sustancia que un organismo necesita para vivir. Ejemplos incluyen agua, minerales y sustancias que provienen de la descomposición de partículas de alimento.

O

organism
An individual living thing, made up of one or many cells, that is capable of growing and reproducing.

organismo Un individuo vivo, compuesto de una o muchas células, que es capaz de crecer y reproducirse.

P, Q

parasitism (PAR-uh-suh-TIHZ-uhm)
A relationship between two species in which one species is harmed while the other benefits; a type of symbiosis. (p. 59)

parasitismo Una relación entre dos especies en la cual una especie es perjudicada mientras que la otra se beneficia; un tipo de simbiosis.

photosynthesis (FOH-toh-SIHN-thih-sihs)
The process by which green plants and other producers use simple compounds and energy from light to make sugar, an energy-rich compound.

> **fotosíntesis** El proceso mediante el cual las plantas verdes y otros productores usan compuestos simples y energía de la luz para producir azúcares, compuestos ricos en energía.

pioneer species
The first species to move into a lifeless environment. Plants like mosses are typical pioneer species on land. (p. 66)

> **especie pionera** La primera especie que ocupa un medio ambiente sin vida. Las plantas como los musgos son típicas especies pioneras terrestres.

pollution
The release of harmful substances into the air, water, or land. (p. 91)

> **contaminación** La descarga de sustancias nocivas al aire, al agua o a la tierra.

population
A group of organisms of the same species that live in the same area. For example, a desert will have populations of different species of lizards and cactus plants. (p. 46)

> **población** Un grupo de organismos de la misma especie que viven en la misma área. Por ejemplo, un desierto tendrá poblaciones de distintas especies de lagartijas y de cactus.

population density
A measure of the number of organisms that live in a given area. The population density of a city may be given as the number of people living in a square kilometer. (p. 86)

> **densidad de población** Una medida de la cantidad de organismos que viven un área dada. La densidad de población de una ciudad puede expresarse como el número de personas que viven en un kilómetro cuadrado.

predator
An animal that hunts other animals and eats them. An owl is a predator that feeds on small animals such as mice. (p. 55)

> **predador** Un animal que caza otros animales y se los come. Un búho es un predador que se alimenta de animales pequeños como los ratones.

prey
An animal that other animals hunt and eat. A mouse is prey that is eaten by other animals, such as owls and snakes. (p. 55)

> **presa** Un animal que otros animales cazan y se comen. Un ratón es una presa que es comido por otros animales como los búhos y las serpientes.

producer
An organism that captures energy from sunlight and transforms it into chemical energy that is stored in energy-rich carbon compounds. Producers are a source of food for other organisms. (p. 23)

> **productor** Un organismo que capta energía de la luz solar y la transforma a energía química que se almacena en compuestos de carbono ricos en energía. Los productores son una fuente de alimento para otros organismos.

R, S

respiration
The physical and chemical processes by which a living thing exchanges gases with the environment. In cellular respiration, cells take in oxygen and release the energy stored in carbon compounds.

> **respiración** Los procesos físicos y químicos mediante los cuales un organismo vivo toma oxígeno y libera energía. En la respiración celular, las células absorben oxígeno y liberan la energía almacenada en compuestos de carbono.

species
A group of living things that are so closely related that they can breed with one another and produce offspring that can breed as well. (p. 45)

> **especie** Un grupo de organismos que están tan estrechamente relacionados que pueden aparearse entre sí y producir crías que también pueden aparearse.

succession (suhk-SEHSH-uhn)
A natural process that involves a gradual change in the plant and animal communities that live in an area. (p. 66)

> **sucesión** Un proceso natural que involucra un cambio gradual en las comunidades de plantas y animales que viven en un área.

sustainable
A term that describes the managing of certain natural resources so that they are not harmed or used up. Examples include maintaining clean groundwater and protecting top soil from erosion. (p. 102)

> **sostenible** Un término que describe el manejo de ciertos recursos naturales para que no se deterioren o se terminen. Ejemplos incluyen mantener limpia el agua subterránea y proteger de la erosión a la capa superficial del suelo.

symbiosis (SIHM-bee-OH-sihs)
The interaction between individuals from two different species that live closely together. (p. 58)

> **simbiosis** La interacción entre individuos de dos especies distintas que viven en proximidad.

system
A group of objects or phenomena that interact. A system can be as simple as a rope, a pulley, and a mass. It also can be as complex as the interaction of energy and matter in the four spheres of the Earth system.

> **sistema** Un grupo de objetos o fenómenos que interactúan. Un sistema puede ser algo tan sencillo como una cuerda, una polea y una masa. También puede ser algo tan complejo como la interacción de la energía y la materia en las cuatro esferas del sistema de la Tierra.

T

technology
The use of scientific knowledge to solve problems or engineer new products, tools, or processes.

> **tecnología** El uso de conocimientos científicos para resolver problemas o para diseñar nuevos productos, herramientas o procesos.

theory
In science, a set of widely accepted explanations of observations and phenomena. A theory is a well-tested explanation that is consistent with all available evidence.

> **teoría** En las ciencias, un conjunto de explicaciones de observaciones y fenómenos que es ampliamente aceptado. Una teoría es una explicación bien probada que es consecuente con la evidencia disponible.

U

urban
A term that describes a city environment.

> **urbano** Un término que describe el medio ambiente de una ciudad.

V

variable
Any factor that can change in a controlled experiment, observation, or model. (p. R30)

> **variable** Cualquier factor que puede cambiar en un experimento controlado, en una observación o en un modelo.

volume
An amount of three-dimensional space, often used to describe the space that an object takes up.

> **volumen** Una cantidad de espacio tridimensional; a menudo se usa este término para describir el espacio que ocupa un objeto.

W, X, Y, Z

water cycle
The continuous movement of water through Earth, its atmosphere, and the living things on Earth. (p. 17)

> **ciclo del agua** El movimiento continuo de agua por la Tierra, su atmósfera y los organismos vivos de la Tierra.

Index

Page numbers for definitions are printed in **boldface** type.
Page numbers for illustrations, maps, and charts are printed in *italics*.

INDEX

M

manufacturing and pollution, 92
marine biomes, 35, 36–37, *37*, 38
marsh ecosystems, 36. *See also* aquatic biomes.
mass transit, *104*
math skills
    adding integers, 21
    area, **R43**
    decimal, **R39**, R40
    describing a set of data, R36–R37
    formulas, **R42**
    fractions, *69*, **R41**
    mean, **R36**
    median, **R36**
    mode, **R37**
    multiplying fractions by whole numbers, *69*
    percents, **R41**
    proportions, **R39**
    range, **R37**
    rates, **R38**
    ratios, **R38**
    scientific notation, **R44**
    significant figures, **R44**
    volume, *97,* **R43**
Mather, Stephen, 75
mating, competition within species, 56
mean, **R36**
median, **R36**
metal as natural resource, 84
metric system, R20–R21
    changing metric units, R20, *R20*
    converting between U.S. customary units, R21, *R21*
    temperature conversion, R21, *R21*
microorganisms as biotic factors, 10
microscope, R14–R15, *R14*
    making a slide or wet mount, R15, *R15*
    viewing an object, R15
minerals, 13, 84, 91
mode, **R37**
moose, population patterns, 64
mosses, 31, 66
Muir, John, 75
mutualism, **58**, *58, 60, 70*

N

National Environmental Policy Act (U.S. law), 100
National Park Service, 75
national parks, *75,* 98–99
natural gas, 91, 104
natural resources, **84,** 84–87
Nature Conservancy, 4, 76
nest parasitism, *61*
niche, **47,** 70

nitrogen
    atmospheric, 19, *20*
    cycle, **19,** 19–20, *20,* 38
    fixation, 19, *20,* 60
nitrogen dioxide, 92
nitrogen-fixing bacteria, 19, *20, 60*
    and alder trees, 68
    and alfalfa, 19
    and soybeans, 19
nonrenewable resources, 89–91, *90,* 103, 104
note-taking strategies, R45–R49
    combination notes, *8,* R45, *R45*
    concept map, R49, *R49*
    content frame, R45, *R45*
    main idea and detail notes, R46, *R46*
    main idea web, R46, *R46*
    mind map, R47, *R47*
    outline, *44,* R48, *R48*
    supporting main ideas, *80,* R47, *R47*
    Venn diagram, R49, *R49*

O

oasis, *13*
observations, **xxiv, R2,** R5, R33
    qualitative, R2
    quantitative, R2
ocean ecosystems, 36–37. *See also* marine biomes.
    commensalism in, *59*
oil, *90,* 104
open ocean biome, 36, *37*
operational definition, **R31**
opinion, *R9*
organisms, **xv.** *See also* living things.
    groupings of, within ecosystems, 45–48, *49*
    interaction of, 54–61, 70
organization
    cells and, xv
    living things and, xv
oxygen, xvii, 17

P, Q

parasitism, **59,** *60, 61, 70*
percents, **R41**
permafrost, 31
pesticides, 29, 76
petroleum, 91
photosynthesis, 12, 13, 22. *See also* producers.
    by algae, *18*
    carbon cycle and, *18*
    by plants, *18*
phytoplankton, 35, 36
    as producers, *23,* 35, 36
Pinchot, Gifford, 75

Acknowledgments

Photography

Cover © Richard du Toit/Nature Picture Library; **iii** Photograph of James Trefil by Evan Cantwell; Photograph of Rita Ann Calvo by Joseph Calvo; Photograph of Kenneth Cutler by Kenneth A. Cutler; Photograph of Douglas Carnine by McDougal Littell; Photograph of Linda Carnine by Amilcar Cifuentes; Photograph of Donald Steely by Marni Stamm; Photograph of Sam Miller by Samuel Miller; Photograph of Vicky Vachon by Redfern Photographics; **vi** © Jeff Schultz/Alaska Stock.com; **vii** © Wolcott Henry/National Geographic Image Collection; **ix** *bottom left* © David Young-Wolff/PhotoEdit, Inc.; *top right, bottom right* Photographs by Ken O'Donoghue; **xiv, xv** © Mark Hamblin/Age Fotostock; **xvi, xvii** © Georgette Duowma/Taxi/Getty Images; **xviii, xix** © Ron Sanford/Corbis; **xx, xxi** © Nick Vedros & Assoc./Stone/Getty Images; **xxii** © Dr. Ken MacDonald/Science Photo Library/Photo Researchers, Inc.; **xxii** *left* © Michael Gadomski/Animals Animals; *right* © Shin Yoshino/Minden Pictures; **xxiii** © Laif Elleringmann/Aurora Photos; **xxiv** © Pascal Goetgheluck/Science Photo Library/Photo Researchers, Inc.; **xxv** *top left* © David Parker/Science Photo Library/Photo Researchers, Inc.; *top right* © James King-Holmes/Science Photo Library/Photo Researchers, Inc.; *bottom* Sinsheimer Labs/University of California, Santa Cruz; **xxvi, xxvii** *background* © Maximillian Stock/Photo Researchers, Inc.; **xxvi** *top* © John Lair, Jewish Hospital, University of Louisville; **xxvii** *top* © Brand X Pictures/Alamy; *center* Courtesy, AbioMed; **xxxii** © Chedd-Angier Production Company; **2, 3** *background* © Mark Thiessen/National Geographic Image Collection; **3** *top* © Frank Oberle/Getty Images; *bottom* © Hal Horwitz/Corbis; **4** *top (both)* © Lawrence J. Godson; *bottom* Chedd-Angier Production Company; **6, 7** © Jeff Schultz/Alaska Stock.com; **7** *top* Photograph by Ken O'Donoghue; *center* Photograph by Frank Siteman; **9** Photograph by Frank Siteman; **10** © Mark Allen Stack/Tom Stack & Associates; **11** *left* © Jim Brandenburg/Minden Pictures; *right* © Ted Kerasote/Photo Researchers, Inc.; **12** *bottom left* © Grant Heilman Photography; **13** © Frans Lemmens/Getty Images; **14** *top* © Michael J. Doolittle/The Image Works, Inc.; *bottom* Photograph by Ken O'Donoghue; **16** Photograph by Ken O'Donoghue; **19** Photograph by Frank Siteman; **21** © Randy Wells/Corbis; **22** Photograph by Frank Siteman; **23** *left* © Eric Crichton/Corbis; *top right* © E.R. Degginger/Color-Pic, Inc.; *bottom right* © T.E. Adams/Visuals Unlimited, Inc.; **24** © Anthony Mercieca Photo/Photo Researchers, Inc.; **25** *top* © Fred Bruemmer/DRK Photo; *bottom* Photograph by Ken O'Donoghue; **27** *background* © Raymond Gehman/Corbis; **29** *left* © Arthur Gurmankin & Mary Morina/Visuals Unlimited, Inc.; *top right* © Carmela Leszczynski/Animals Animals; **30** © Charles Melton/Visuals Unlimited, Inc.; **31** © Michio Hoshino/Minden Pictures; **32** *top left* © Tom Bean; *top right* © E.R. Degginger/Color-Pic, Inc.; *bottom* © Joe McDonald/Visuals Unlimited, Inc.; **33** *left* © David Wrobel/Visuals Unlimited, Inc.; *right* © Tom Bean; **34** *left* © Owaki-Kulla/Corbis; *right* © Frans Lanting/Minden Pictures; **35** *top* Photograph by Ken O'Donoghue; *bottom* © Stephen Dalton/Photo Researchers, Inc.; **36** *left* © Aaron Horowitz/Corbis; *center* © Hans Pfletschinger/Peter Arnold, Inc.; *right* © Arthur Gurmankin & Mary Morina/Visuals Unlimited, Inc.; **37** *left* © Paul Rezendes; *center* © Richard Herrmann/Visuals Unlimited, Inc.; *right* © Norbert Wu; **42, 43** © Wolcott Henry/National Geographic Image Collection; **43** *top* Photograph by Frank Siteman; *center* Photograph by Ken O'Donoghue; **45** Photograph by Frank Siteman; **46** *left and center* © Frans Lanting/Minden Pictures; *right* © Robin Karpan/Visuals Unlimited, Inc.; **50** © Walt Anderson/Visuals Unlimited, Inc.; **51** ©Alan & Linda Detrick/Photo Researchers, Inc.; **52** *top* © Patrick J. Endres/Visuals Unlimited, Inc.; *bottom left* Photograph by Frank Siteman; *bottom right* Photograph by Ken O'Donoghue; **53** Photograph by Ken O'Donoghue; **54** © Spencer Grant/PhotoEdit, Inc.; **55** © Gary Braasch; **56** *top* © Joe McDonald/Visuals Unlimited, Inc.; *bottom* © Stephen J. Krasemann/Photo Researchers, Inc.; **57** *top* Photograph by Ken O'Donoghue; *bottom* © Michael Fogden/Bruce Coleman Inc.; **58** © Michael & Patricia Fogden/Minden Pictures; **59** © Bradley Sheard; **60** *clockwise from top* © S.J. Krasemann/Peter Arnold, Inc.; © Ray Coleman/Visuals Unlimited, Inc.; © Astrid & Hanns-Frieder Michler/Science Photo Library; © E.R. Degginger/Color-Pic, Inc.; © Dwight R. Kuhn; © Phil Degginger/Color-Pic, Inc.; **61** © Arthur Morris/Visuals Unlimited, Inc.; **62** *left* © Kevin Fleming/Corbis; *inset* © David M. Dennis/Animals Animals; **63** Photograph by Ken O'Donoghue; **64** *top* © Shin Yoshino/Minden Pictures; *bottom* © Tim Fitzharris/Minden Pictures; **65** Photograph by Frank Siteman; **66** *bottom (background)* © Leo Collier/Getty Images; **67** *bottom (background)* © David R. Frazier/Getty Images; **69** © A. & J. Visage/Peter Arnold, Inc.; **70** *top left* © Frans Lanting/Minden Pictures; **74** *bottom center* Denver Public Library, Western History Collection, call#F-4659; *top center* © James Randklev/Getty Images; *bottom right* Library of Congress, Prints and Photographs Division (LC-USZ62-16709 DLC) cph 3a18915; **75** *top left* © H.H. French/Corbis; *top right* © Bill Ross/Corbis; *center left* The Bancroft Library, University of California, Berkeley; *center right* © Corbis; *bottom* © Michael Sewell/Peter Arnold, Inc.; **76** *top left* © Alfred Eisenstaedt/Getty Images; *top right* © Tom Bean/DRK Photo; *center right* © David Muench/Corbis; *bottom left* © Kevin Schafer/Corbis; *bottom right* Habitat Quality for San Joaquin Kit Fox on Managed and Private Lands reprinted from ESRI Map Book, Vol. 16 and used herein with permission. Copyright © 2001 ESRI. All rights reserved.; **77** *top* © Tom Soucek/Alaska Stock Images; *bottom* © Richard Galosy/Bruce Coleman, Inc.; **78, 79** ©Alex Maclean/Photonica; **79** *top and center* Photographs by Ken O'Donoghue; **81** Photograph by Frank Siteman; **83** © Ray Pfortner/Peter Arnold, Inc.; **84** Photograph by Ken O'Donoghue; **85** *top* © John Elk III; *bottom* © Ted Spiegel/Corbis; **86** *background* © ChromoSohm/Sohm/Photo Researchers, Inc.; *insets* Courtesy, USGS: EROS Data Center; **87** © Mark E. Gibson/Visuals Unlimited, Inc.; **88** © David Zimmerman/Corbis; **89** © David Young-Wolff/PhotoEdit, Inc.; **90** *left* © Richard Stockton/Iguazu Falls/Index Stock Imagery, Inc.; *right* © Bill Ross/Corbis; **91** Photograph by Ken O'Donoghue; **92** *bottom* © Tom Bean/DRK Photo; *inset* © Jenny Hager/The Image Works, Inc.; **93** *bottom* © Natalie Fobes/Corbis; *inset* © Natalie Fobes/Getty Images; **95** © Kent Foster Photgraphs/Visuals Unlimited, Inc.; **96** *top* © Andrew J. Martinez/Photo Researchers, Inc.; *inset* © D. Cavagnaro/Visuals Unlimited, Inc.; **97** © Tom Edwards/Visuals Unlimited, Inc.; **98** Photographs by Ken O'Donoghue and Frank Siteman; **99** © Frank Pedrick/The Image Works, Inc.; **100** © Joe McDonald/Visuals Unlimited, Inc.; **101** *top (background)* © Jim Wark/Airphoto; *top (inset)* Photograph by Scott Williams/U.S. Fish and Wildlife Service; *bottom (background)* © Tom Bean/Corbis; *bottom (insets)* Courtesy, San Diego State University, Soil Ecology and Restoration Group; **102** © Melissa Farlow/National Geographic Image Collection; **103** © Klein/Hubert/Peter Arnold, Inc.; **104** © Janis Miglavs; *bottom* © David Young-Wolff/PhotoEdit, Inc.; **105** © Kevin Schafer/Corbis; **106** *top* Tom Myers/Photo Researchers, Inc.; *bottom* Photograph by Frank Siteman; **108** *center left* © Natalie Fobes/Corbis; *center right* © Kent Foster Photographs/Visuals Unlimited, Inc.; *bottom left* © Joe McDonald/Visuals Unlimited, Inc.; *bottom right* © Klein/Hubert/Peter Arnold, Inc; **R28** © PhotoDisc/Getty Images.

Illustration & Maps

Richard Bonson/Wildlife Art Ltd. **viii, 28, 47, 49, 60** *(background)*, **70** *(top right)*
Sandra Doyle/Wildlife Art Ltd. **27** *(all)*, **38** *(bottom)*
Luigi Galante **66–67** *(all insets)*, **70** *(bottom)*
Dan Gonzalez **88, 94**
Gary Hincks **12** *(bottom right)*, **17, 18, 20, 36–37** *(background)*, **38** *(center)*, **83**
MapQuest.com, Inc. **31, 47** *(top right)*, **49** *(top)*, **85**
Laurie O'Keefe **29**
Dan Stuckenschneider/Uhl Studios **R11–R19, R22, R32**